HOW TO
TEACH
YOUR
CHILD
TO
READ

from two years

clock

car

pig

tree

HOW TO
TEACH
YOUR
CHILD
TO
READ

from two years

Over 125 activities for rapid reading progress

BILL GILLHAM

WARD LOCK

A WARD LOCK BOOK

First published in the UK 1998 by
Ward Lock
Wellington House
125 Strand
London
WC2R 0BB

A Cassell imprint

Reprinted 1999

British Library Cataloguing-in-Publication Data

A catalogue record for this book is available from the British Library

ISBN 0-7063-7757-5

Designed by Suzanne Perkins/Grafica
Illustrations by Peter Ware
Edited by Nikky Twyman

Printed and bound in Great Britain by the Bath Press, Bath

Contents

Introduction

FROM TWO YEARS? Surely that's a misprint for *five* years?

Not at all. The research evidence is clear: a child's future reading progress is almost fifty per cent determined by the time they enter school. And a child who isn't reading by the age of eight has only about a ten per cent chance of leaving school literate.

The convention is that the average 9-year-old has achieved basic literacy. The present book contains activities up to the 8-year level. If your child can read the test passage on page 15 with fewer than five errors, then they're beyond that level and you probably don't need this book. But many older children are not up to that level or are weak in one particular area; and younger children usually need some support teaching if they are to maintain progress.

Current controversy as to how reading should be taught in schools (for example, phonics or not, reading schemes versus 'real' books) misses the point. Different methods produce much the same results on average. The big difference is made by parents developing their children's literacy skills preschool, and providing practice, encouragement and teaching when they're at school. What children need is more *time* on reading and more *individual* help. In the main it is only parents who can provide that, although individual help in school targeted on failing readers in the second year of primary school can have a big effect. But that is difficult to organize and can be expensive to provide. You can't be sure that's going to happen in your child's school. Schools *can* make a big difference, but often they're struggling with too many children who are too far back.

If the preschool stage is so important, why wait until two years of age? The answer is that you don't: you just leave anything like deliberate teaching until then.

Babies need books

At some point between the age of six to nine months, babies start to be captured by vividly coloured picture books. Having an adult turn over the pages is pure magic for a baby; and they soon want to do it for themselves. Whether sitting on someone's knee or turning over the pages on the floor, the baby is learning about books – how to handle them and what you find in them.

Adults are important because they can guide and interpret for the child: talking about the pictures, pointing things out, linking what happens in the book to what happens in the child's world. And it is not just a matter of 'looking at the pictures'. Young children can take in a lot of language from books even if they can't speak much. Psychologists have shown, for example, that children can *understand* fifty words before they can *speak* ten. And reading is about understanding words.

Even though babies aren't able to follow a story, they may respond to storybooks – to the illustrations, or the characters and the things that happen in the story, or because they like the sound or rhythm of the words. Once they begin to be able to link ideas together, then storybooks come into their own. At around the age of eighteen months they start to show signs of noticing printed words – the very beginning of reading.

Reading is a *natural* activity; as natural as talking. There are parts of the brain as specialized for written language as there are for spoken language. It is not just an artificial 'school' accomplishment. Nor does it demand a high IQ in preschoolers. Precocious readers are often intellectually average. And Down's children sometimes start to read at the age of three or four. *Reading isn't much to do with intelligence*: you can have high-IQ children who are very poor readers and low-IQ children who are good readers. So if your child doesn't find reading easy that doesn't mean they're lacking in intelligence. It does mean they need you to help them, and often just a little teaching will set them going.

The trouble is you can 'avoid' written words in a way that you can't avoid spoken words (unless you're deaf). What young children need is a sensitive partner – someone who will introduce them to books and words, and respond to their interest.

Do all children need to be taught to read?

The simple answer is no, or just a little bit of help here and there.

The basis of learning to read is an adult and a young child

sharing a favourite book. For some children it is all they need. They pick up reading without any formal teaching at all.

But most children need *some* simple teaching. Parents may read regularly to their children, buy them books, and yet still find that when their children start school they have difficulty learning to read. A love of books and stories is not a guarantee of literacy, even if it is the main purpose of reading.

Isn't there a danger of pressurizing children?

Of course – but you have to be pretty insensitive to do that. And parents, on the whole, are more sensitive to their children than anyone. In any case, the main danger comes from neglecting children's reading development. A few basic rules will avoid any risk of 'over-teaching' (see p. 20).

How to use this book

This book is no 'pressure' reading programme; it doesn't need to be. Learning to read is natural, enjoyable – and, taken at the right pace, easy.

The reading activities are divided up into three parts:

- Stories and Reading for Meaning

- Words

- Sounds and Letters.

The most important *Top Ten* activities are listed on the first page of each part, along with the page where they can be found.

The approximate *age level* is given for each activity. You will probably be able to tell which activities your child could do at the moment, but you can also assess their present reading level by using the checklists and tests that follow.

To begin with, pick one Top Ten activity from each of the three parts, and another one or two in reserve. A few pointers:

- There are many more activities than you need so choose those that suit your child's present level and personality.

- Aim for variety. Have three or four activities on the go at any one time, changing from one to the other to hold the child's interest.

- Some activities have a longer life than others (especially those in the Top Ten). Drop any activities that don't work for your child and, in any case, replace one activity every week or so with a new one – even if it's just doing the same thing in a different way.

- Keep it short. Five to ten minutes is quite long enough for a young child to spend on any one activity. And the whole session shouldn't last more than twenty to thirty minutes at the outside. Children can learn a lot in just ten to fifteen minutes if they're really interested.

- Finish the session while they're still interested, saying, 'We'll do more of that tomorrow.' Little and often is the rule.

Check your child's literacy level

- For children from two to five you don't test them – you simply check off what they can do on the checklist that follows. This will show you their approximate present level.

- For children aged six, seven and eight there are three graded storybook pages. A simple error-count tells you at what level they can read – but it's usually obvious. The basic rule is that if they get more than one word in ten wrong they can't read independently at that level. If they get more than one word in five wrong it's too difficult even if you're hearing them read and helping them. *Children who are given books they have to struggle with soon get discouraged.*

- Whatever your child's *actual* age, you choose activities at their *reading level* age. So if your 6-year-old child can't manage the 6-year-level test passage, then give them the 5-year-level activities. But as they improve, go on to the more challenging activities.

Literacy checklist 2–5 years

You can't really be sure of a child's reading ability until they reach the age when they can attempt a simple book. But you can observe the early signs of prereading. This checklist will give you some idea of your child's present level.

Age level (years)	Stories and reading for meaning	Words	Sounds and letters
2	• Is 'held' by a simple story when you read it • Asks for a favourite story	• Looks out for printed words – on signs, in books • Shows you where the printed words are in books	• Enjoys nursery rhymes • Can play simple shape-matching games
3	• Talks to you about what happens in stories • Relates stories to real events ('That's like . . .')	• Recognizes familiar logos (like McDonald's) • Asks you to write words (on drawings, for example)	• Notices some letters in words • Finishes off rhymes for you
4	• Pretend reads – makes up a story from pictures • Tells *you* a favourite story	• Picks out some words in familiar books • Writes their own name	• Plays I Spy • Copies over letters
5	• 'Reads' a memorized story quite accurately • Predicts what's going to happen in a story you read to them	• Recognizes a number of words quite independently • Can write a *few* words and copies words	• Tells you what sound words start with • Can write most letters without a copy

How to use these tests

Don't use them with children under six years of age.

- Whatever the child's age, start with 'Billy and the Lion' (6-year level).

- Explain to the child that you want them to read the story for you but you'll tell them any words they don't know.

- Ask them to read the title first and treat this as part of the story as well.

- If the child makes a mistake, give them the correct word: if they stick, wait three seconds (one – pause – two – pause – three) and then give them the word. All of these instances count as errors.

- If they make fewer than *five* errors, go on to the next passage, 'Space Walk' (7-year level); and if they make fewer than five errors on that story, go on to 'Who Believes in Ghosts?' (8-year level).

- A child who makes fewer than five errors at the 8-year level can *read*, but needs lots of practice reading whatever books appeal to them.

- Children who make between five and ten errors on any of the stories need further reading practice and reading activities *at that age level*.

- Children who make ten to fifteen errors need the reading activities a year below that age level and plenty of help with the errors they make in reading (see p. 28).

If you give these tests when you start teaching you can retest six months later to see what progress has been made. Don't retest earlier than that or you'll make the child 'test-conscious' – it's a guide for you, not a *worry* for them.

Billy and the Lion

'There's a lion in my bed,' said Billy.

'Don't be silly,' said Mum.

'Go to bed,' said Dad.

Billy went upstairs to bed.

The lion ate him up, all of him.

Then the lion came downstairs.

'Roar!' went the lion.

'That's just Billy,' said Mum.

'Pretending to be a lion,' said Dad.

But they were wrong.

Weren't they?

Space Walk

It was time for the space walk. Ross put on his space suit. He slid into the air lock. He had to fix the damage to the spaceship. He hooked on the rope that kept him safe. The tools hung from his belt.

He waited. The door opened. He was out in space.

He worked for an hour. All around him empty space. He tried not to think about it.

Off came the damaged part. The rest was easy. Done at last.

'OK?' said the captain as he slid back into the spaceship.

'Easy,' said Ross.

Who Believes in Ghosts?

Karen didn't believe in ghosts. That was why she had come all alone to the old house.

Everything was quiet. Pale moonlight filtered through the dirty windows. Dust and broken furniture were everywhere.

What was that scratching noise? Probably rats. Karen shivered. In the distance a door banged. The whole house echoed like a drum. She heard footsteps coming slowly along the passage.

'I'm not scared,' Karen whispered to herself, 'there's nothing there.'

Slowly the door opened; a hand appeared round the corner. Karen screamed.

'Karen,' said her dad, 'don't be silly and come on home.'

Introduction

PART I
Stories and Reading for Meaning

top
ten

Sharing a Book

Children learn a lot from sharing a book with an adult, becoming increasingly involved. The following hints are in age-level order, with the easiest first. You have to judge what you can expect your child to do.

- *Ask your child to find where the story starts.* Finding the beginning of the book and where the words start is an important step in itself. By showing *you* they're showing themselves.

- *Point to the words as you're reading.* Not laboriously, word by word – just run your finger left to right along the line. That helps the child to notice the words and the reading direction.

- *Ask them to turn the pages for you.* This makes them pay attention to the spoken word/written word link-up and 'involves' them.

- *Talk about the pictures to show that they link up with the words.* Pictures prompt the words and the story – children need to learn this.

- *Talk about the story to help them understand it better.* A good way of doing this is to link the incidents and characters to events and people in the child's own life, e.g. 'Do you remember when Katie did that?'

- *Ask them to tell you what's going to happen next in a story, before you turn over the page.* This is a key skill, basic to literacy. Part of the pleasure of stories is the unexpected (and something's unexpected because you expected – or *predicted* – something else).

- *When they are familiar with a book, ask them to tell you the story, turning over the pages with the pictures as a prompt.* It doesn't matter if their story doesn't exactly match the story in the printed words. They are constructing a story and *getting the story idea.*

THE GOLDEN RULES

- *Plan* your teaching sessions, but be flexible in response to how your child reacts to what you're teaching.

- Have at least three activities ready, and one or two as alternatives, so that you can switch if necessary.

- Pick *very different* activities, so there's plenty of variety in any one session.

- Drop any activities that don't work for your child, and replace them with something else – there's plenty of choice. Remember, there's more than one way of teaching the same skill.

- Bring in new activities regularly, anyway, so the sessions don't get 'samey'.

- Don't continue for longer than half an hour; much less than that with children under five, *unless* they are desperate to continue. Even very young children can be amazingly persistent when they are really interested.

- If they *are* losing interest, wrap the session up smartly. Don't try to 'persuade' them. Ten minutes when they're really concentrating and 'involved' is worth more than half an hour when you have to coax them along.

- Make sure the activities are neither too easy (when they'll get bored) or too *hard* (when they'll get discouraged). Children need to feel challenged *and* competent.

- Pick a time of day when you can be free of distractions – and make sure other members of the family know that you're trying to do something.

The Library Habit

Good habits start young. Some children grow up without being used to visiting the library regularly. It's an unfamiliar place, not part of their world. So if you want your child to be a good reader it's worth making a deliberate effort to drop in whenever you're in that area shopping, and to change your own library books.

Modern libraries with 'dip-in' boxes allow very young children to get their hands on a wide variety of books. It also means that they can discover books *they* like. Strong favourites can be bought and added to the child's own permanent collection.

Librarians know how important 'the library habit' is. Introduce your child to the staff – make it more personal.

Storytelling

Stories don't exist in books: they exist in our heads. Whether reading it for themselves, or having it read to them, the child has to reconstruct the story in their own mind to understand it. Understanding stories is an important stage not just in learning to read but also in the child's language and intellectual development.

Encouraging a child to *tell* stories (made up or taken from books) is an excellent way of learning about story language. Ask them to tell a bedtime story to you or to a doll or teddy bear.

Read it again!

An important part of learning to read is the constant rereading of favourite books. But it isn't just a matter of repeating the pleasure of hearing a well-loved story: each time the child gets a better understanding of what the story is about, and what stories are about in general.

Drawing a Story

Read a story aloud, then encourage the child to draw what appeals to them in the story.

Children will sometimes do this spontaneously, usually picking on one vivid incident or main character or collapsing several bits of a story into one big picture. It may not be quite 'logical' but it helps develop their skill in re-presenting the story in a way they perhaps couldn't do in words.

Acting a Story

This is something young children enjoy hugely, especially if there is a bit of dressing up and you join in – which means that you can prompt and help the story along. Again this is something that children will do spontaneously, but adult help (not control) often makes it more successful.

Sophie is not yet three but has already shown that her reading is, in some areas, at the age-five level.

She has half a dozen storybooks that she has practised reading together with her father: this is largely memorizing but she clearly gets something from the print and has identified some of the words in other books – real word recognition.

She has started to produce recognizable drawings and these have gone into her word book: those words she can read independently without the picture.

She is left-handed and finds copying over letters troublesome, often getting the direction wrong. This was a surprise to her father but he has put it to one side for the moment.

Sophie easily works for almost half an hour (and demands more), but her father thinks that's enough. A typical session for her might include:

• share-reading a new storybook (p. 19)

• Matching Words to Words Under Pictures (p. 60)

• Matching Sets of Pictures by Their Initial-Letter Sounds (p. 105).

ESTABLISHING A ROUTINE

The word *routine* suggests something boring and restrictive. After all, if learning to read is a basically natural process then shouldn't teaching be spontaneous and casual?

You can have those important elements in a routine that supports learning. Young children have to learn *how* to learn – the habits that make learning easier.

If you go into the intake class of a primary school, the most striking thing is the orderly way children go about their activities. Their teachers spend a lot of time establishing clear rules and good habits. Children won't learn without them. Young children *like* routine: it's reassuring for them (and it's reassuring for us). And if they know what to expect in how you arrange your teaching sessions they'll be able to concentrate on the *content* of the session – which is what really matters.

A few tips:

■ Pick a regular time of day when you're not harassed and they're at their best (let's hope they coincide!).

■ Keep the materials for the activities you're using in a box (a box file is ideal).

■ Have a regular *place* (on the coffee table or wherever) where you and the child play the games.

■ Make sure *you* have a clear plan of what you're going to teach in the session.

■ Get one activity at a time out of the box and tidy it away before you go on to the next one.

■ If the child doesn't cooperate, don't go on about it: just wrap things up. The odds are that the next day they'll be setting out the box ready for you.

years

Picture-Card Storytelling

You can either draw the pictures yourself (children like to watch!) or cut pictures out of a comic or magazine. Start with no more than three cards. For example:

Put the cards in order and, pointing to the first one, ask: 'What's happening here?' Move on to the second: 'Then what happened?'; and then the third: 'What happened in the end?'

You can develop this activity in two ways: first, by using more cards and, second, by showing that you can tell *different* stories using the *same* cards.

BOOKS OF THEIR OWN

Having their own books doesn't necessarily make children good readers but, in general, the more books children have *just for themselves*, the better they are going to be at reading. Young children have very strong feelings about ownership – it's one of the first things they talk about. They'll like a little bookcase for 'their' books.

You could join a children's book club – these are listed on p. 126. Children like getting things through the post, and choosing books from the catalogue and waiting for them to arrive are all part of the fun.

Going to a bookshop can become a special treat for the child – another part of the 'book' habit.

What Happens Next?

Here you have a set of picture cards that tell a story but *the last one is missing*. You ask the child to tell you the story from the cards that *are* there and get them to *guess* what happened at the end. (You can then produce the final card – it doesn't matter if their version of the story is different, so long as it 'fits'.)

Jumbled Picture-Card Stories

This is a real challenge that children enjoy. You present the picture cards that tell a story (as on the previous page), *but they're in the wrong order*. A three-card set is quite difficult enough to begin with. Set the cards out in jumbled order and say: 'There's a story on these cards but they're in the wrong order. Can you put them in the right order to tell the story?'

Don't let them struggle. If necessary, *show* them the sequence and talk the story through.

*J*oseph is just over four years of age. A very active child, he doesn't usually settle to any one activity for more than five minutes.

He doesn't like to share a storybook except for one he made up himself, with his mother's help. He likes drawing and can copy over letters well with just a little guidance. His word book is full of pictures of animals all drawn by himself.

A typical session for Joseph (using the kind of activities he likes) is:

• 'reading' his Do-it-Yourself Book (p. 26)

• practising writing his own name (p. 58)

• playing Words Across the Room (p. 61).

This last game is deliberately a very 'physical' one – Joseph wouldn't be satisfied just to sit at a table to do the same kind of thing.

years

Do-it-Yourself Books

'It's time to get up!'

'I don't feel well!' said Katie.

Books, no matter how home-made, have a special fascination for children if their own words are used. You can use family photos or drawings (yours or the child's). It doesn't have to be a storybook; just a picture with a line of text underneath will satisfy most very young children. But it's easy to make a simple story with a series of drawings. You can either draw the outlines, which the child can colour in, or encourage them to do their own pictures.

Very young children will just want to make a series of unconnected drawings. Older ones will be able to be able to make a story that links up – which can be 'real life' or made up. Ask them which words should go under each picture, guiding them where necessary. Write the words while they watch, staple the pages together and make a card cover.

This is an activity that can be made as simple or ambitious as you like, to suit the child's level. Young children will get a lot of pleasure out of reading 'their' book to friends and relatives.

Stories and Reading for Meaning

Reading Together

This is something that often occurs naturally. You're rereading a favourite book and the child chimes in and reads with you. They may not be really reading: they've memorized the story (although they usually get something from the print) and, gradually, the words on the page and the words they say come closer together.

Again, quite naturally, they'll tell you to stop reading so that they can do it!

As a technique this is usually called 'paired reading', but, here as elsewhere, technique is overrated as this is essentially a natural stage in learning to read.

A simplified form of paired reading, suitable for young children, is as follows:

The simplified paired reading method

1 Choose a book with only one or two lines to a page and not more than twenty-four pages (even fewer than that to begin with).

2 Tell the child you are *both* going to read the story *at the same time*. To begin with, the child will be hesitant: adjust your speed so that you are reading almost simultaneously, *pointing to the words* as you go.

3 If the child makes a mistake, repeat the correct word – but *keep going*, so that fluency is maintained.

4 Once you and the child are reading together, gradually increase your speed.

5 As the child becomes more confident, lower your voice and, progressively, try dropping out altogether.

6 If the child stumbles or gets stuck, give the correct word and continue 'paired reading' to support fluency, dropping out again quite quickly.

7 Read the story *right through* every two or three days until the child is 'reading' from memory. Real reading follows.

Stories and Reading for Meaning

years

Hearing a Child Read Their Book

Whatever you may think about the story quality in school reading schemes (and the more recent ones are much better), teachers, and children themselves, attach great importance to them.

Your child's 'reader' book is one they will have practised, so they'll appear better at it than on a book of the same level that they haven't seen before. But any difficulties they display are those that really cause them problems.

Points to bear in mind:

- Don't try to take them through the whole book unless it's very short. The little-and-often rule is the key.

- Your job is to give them practice, help them to deal with their mistakes, and understand the story better.

The mistakes children make when they are trying to read independently tell you a lot about their difficulties. You then have to think what particular extra help they need.

Overcoming difficulties

Depending on the kind of mistakes children make, you do different things to help them. Here are the main kinds of things that go wrong and what you do about them:

- *Just can't read the word.* Give them the word, get them to repeat the sentence and then move on. But note the word for some Flash-Card practice (see p. 70). If you focus too much on words they can't read, they'll just give up trying.

- *Reads a word wrongly.* If the word makes sense but doesn't look like the word on the page, say: 'Let's look at that word again.' Read the sentence from the beginning and give the sounds for the first two letters of the word ('The cat sat on the ma...'). If they still don't get it, note the word for Flash-Card practice. If the word *doesn't* make sense, repeat what they've said and say: 'Can that be right? Let's try again.'

Stories and Reading for Meaning

28

- *Mispronouncing words.* Don't make too much fuss about this, but if it's wildly wrong, say: 'That's a difficult one, you say it like this . . .'

- *Reversals.* These are of two kinds: reversing individual letters (reading *b* for *d* (and the other way round) is the most common) and reversing whole words like *was* and *saw*, or parts of words. The important thing to recognize is that these errors are *normal* in young children. The activities on pages 103 and 111 will help.

LEFT TO RIGHT, TOP TO BOTTOM

It's so obvious we don't think about it; it's 'natural'.

Well, it isn't, and children have to learn it. If you are clear about that, you can help them. The rules for reading a book, in English and many other languages, are:

■ You start at the front and go through to the back. (How do you know which is the front?)

■ You read the left-hand page before the right-hand page.

■ You start at the top of the page.

■ You read the lines from left to right.

■ You read every line down to the bottom.

This isn't how you read Arabic, which is read from right to left – perfectly natural for a large part of the human race. So when you're sharing a book with your child talk them through how books work in *their* language.

TALKING LIKE A BOOK?

Psychologists have come to realize that there is a special kind of spoken language – *literate language* – which is basic to school success. This is the ability to talk about things in story form, or *narrative*. The child's experience of stories lays the foundation for this skill, which is quite different from day-to-day social talk with family and friends. Although books and reading are an important part of this skill, there is more to it than that. You don't need books to tell stories and many societies have a strong storytelling tradition without widespread literacy.

WHAT IF YOU FIND YOU CAN'T TEACH YOUR OWN CHILD?

All parents teach their children – good habits, how to behave, everyday skills, special interests and hobbies.

But teaching a child to read is a bit different and you may find that you are both getting upset or angry with each other so that it's not working.

Don't give up immediately. Ask yourself: 'Am I really following the guidelines?' (see p. 20) and 'What am I doing wrong?' It's often something quite simple – like persisting with an activity the child doesn't take to; or not having enough variety in one session; or simply going on for too long.

If you have a conflict, give it a rest for two or three days, think things through and try again.

If you still feel it's not working, think if there's someone else in the family, or a friend, who could do the teaching for you.

The Picture and Answer Game

This game is a good one for children who are not very confident about writing words. Here all they have to do is tick 'Yes' or 'No', *but they have to understand what they read*.

1   Cut out an activity picture from a magazine and mount it at the top of an A4 sheet of paper.

2   Underneath you simply write questions that require a Yes or No answer, e.g.

	Yes	No
Is the car red?	____	____
Is the dog in the car?	____	____

and so on.

Because what they have to *do* is simple, children often don't realize that their reading skill is being stretched.

3   Five or six questions of this type is plenty.

WHAT ABOUT DYSLEXIA?

Most children who are not making sufficient progress in reading simply require efficient teaching – there's nothing complicated about it and they will usually make good progress.

But what about those children who are well taught and yet make poor progress? Whether you call such children dyslexic or not is an academic point. But such children do need help *irrespective of their IQ*. All children – with rare exceptions – should be able to learn to read.

First approach the school psychological service and ask for an educational psychologist to see your child. You can do this directly or through your child's headteacher. You could also approach one of the privately funded bodies concerned with dyslexia (see p. 125).

years

Making a book corner

A child's books are usually confined to their bedroom – not necessarily the best place for reading because bedrooms are often small and not comfortable for sitting. It also means that books are 'out of sight' of day-to-day living.

Why not have a book corner in the living room? You can easily make one out of two low bookcases of laminated chipboard. If two large hinges are fitted to one side, and a large hook and eye to the other, it can be closed up when not in use. And a large cushion or a child's chair can make it more inviting . . .

Hearing Children Read New Books

New to them, that is! Pick books that are not too long (no more than thirty-two pages and, to begin with, no more than eight to twelve pages).

And, more important, books that don't have a lot of words on the page. Less confident readers panic when they see a mass of print (even though they probably could read it). But, if they can see that they only have to read a few words before they're turning the page, they're more likely to try.

If you think they're up to it, start them reading the story to you right away. Concentrate on keeping them going (give them any words they stumble over). They need to feel competent, so support them as unobtrusively as possible. And give them plenty of praise when they've finished!

If you want to ease them into it, you can do it this way:

- Introduce the book, looking through it and asking them what they think it's going to be about from the illustrations.

- Read the story to them *once*, occasionally stopping to ask them about the pictures or to see what they think is going to happen next.

Stories and Reading for Meaning

- When you've finished, close the book and ask them to tell you the story.

- Only *then* ask them to read the story to you. Deal with their errors as before.

Keeping your place

When children are at the word-by-word stage of reading (when they still see reading as something you do out loud), they can easily 'lose their place'. What they usually have to do is to run their finger along the line. Skilled readers are looking ahead of what they're actually saying, but less skilled ones need to focus on where they're at – which is one reason why a lot of print on the page puts them off. If this is the case, it may help them if you cut a piece of card like this:

the cat sat

so they can slide it along the line and expose the words they are reading as they go. It also emphasizes the left-to-right direction, which can also be a problem for inexperienced readers.

This is a prop for the early stages – not for almost-skilled readers.

Stories and Reading for Meaning

years

The Gap Game

This is particularly useful with children who put in words that don't make sense when they are reading. Children who do this are not paying enough attention to the *meaning*.

Children enjoy The Gap Game very much and it *forces* them to think what a missing word should be from the other words that are there.

What you do is quite simple:

1   Photocopy one or more pages from a book at the child's reading level.

2   Using correction fluid, white out words at regular intervals (these are the gaps).

3   You can either white out words at regular intervals (every seventh word is usual) or words at irregular intervals that can be predicted more or less exactly from context. For example, 'She cut herself a _____ of cake and _____ it quickly.'

4   When you've done the whiting out, enlarge the photocopy (by fifty per cent probably).

5   Underline the gaps so that the child can clearly see where they have to put a word in.

6   Explain to them that they have to work out what the missing words are from the ones that are there.

7   You can either ask them to read the passage and *tell* you what the missing words are or they can *write* them in. Because they have to think about it, children usually find it easier to write the word.

8   When they've finished, go through what they've done.

9   If they've put in a completely wrong word, read out the sentence and ask them to think of a word that would fit the sentence better.

Ignore spelling errors at this stage.

Finish the Gap

This is a variation that you can use with slightly younger children or those who find The Gap Game a bit difficult.

You make up the page in exactly the same kind of way, except that you hand-write in the *first two letters* of each missing word followed by a line to show it has to be completed – for example, 'te_____'. This helps the child to predict the word. It also makes them pay attention to the first two letters of a word that they may not know. If you use context and the beginning sounds of a word, you can almost always get it right.

The Picture Gap Game

This game helps children to use illustrations as a prompt for the missing words.

1   Cut an activity picture out of a magazine and stick it to one side of an A4 sheet of paper.

2   Next to it, write sentences that describe the picture with one word missing. For example,

The little girl has a _____ in her hair.

The colour of the bucket is _____.

and so on.

3   They can either *say* the answer or *write* it.

4   If they find it difficult, you can say: 'Look, I'll write the first two letters of the word and you can do the rest.'

The Instruction Game

The rule here is: NO TALKING.

1   Set out four or five objects on a low table – for example, keys, a pencil, a cup, a teddy, a spoon.

2   Write instructions on cards, such as:

Give me the keys.

Give teddy a pencil.

Put the spoon in the cup.

3   If the child can't read a word, prompt with the sound of the first two letters.

Here, the objects are under the child's nose and act as a kind of prompt. To make the game more difficult, the child can be given instructions about things that are out of sight or, at least, that they have to look around for.

1   Prepare four or five cards giving instructions such as:

Go up to your bedroom and bring me down your red T-shirt.

Turn the television on to [channel required].

Bring me a banana out of the kitchen.

2   Prompt any words they can't read, but otherwise NO TALKING.

Children enjoy the activity element in both versions of this game. This is even more true of the next.

Treasure Trail

Hide the 'treasure' (comic, Mars bar, coin, or whatever) at the end of the trail. Then plant a series of instruction cards, one leading on to the other. For example, you hand the child the first card which might say:

In the top drawer in the kitchen

which has another card in it saying:

Under the sponge in the bathroom

and so on. Four or five cards leading to the treasure is enough.

This activity (like some of the others that are more 'physical') is a good way of ending a session.

In my red shoe

Publish Your Own Book

Modern computers and software packages have revolutionized publishing (gone are the days of cumbersome typesetting). It is now perfectly possible to produce quite professional-looking books at home (as many people do).

Children are often computer-literate at a very young age. With the right software, a child's story can be transformed into something that looks like the real thing.

One can overdo the technology, but helping a child to write and produce their own books is an excellent way of developing their literacy as well as giving them a reason for using the family PC. As they become more competent they can go on to more ambitious book-publishing projects.

Activities like this are time-consuming, so they should be seen as an extra to the normal teaching sessions.

Stories and Reading for Meaning

SILENT READING

I have a vivid memory of a time, at the age of seven, when I was sitting in class during a reading period. We were all supposed to be reading our book. The boy next to me was muttering away, laboriously. I was silent and he looked up and said, 'You're not reading!' I insisted I was and ran my eyes along the lines to show him; he wasn't convinced. For him reading was something you did out loud.

When we are teaching children to read it is easy to lose sight of the fact that what we're aiming for is skilled reading which is *silent*. Reading out loud makes reading more difficult for children who are verging on the 'skilled' level – for two reasons:

■ it slows them down (it would slow *you* down), and

■ it distracts attention from the *meaning* of what is being read.

When you feel the child is almost up to the transition point, you can give them books that are *quite easy* for them and say: 'Let's see if you can read these without saying the words out loud.'

The move from reading out loud, word by word, to reading silently for meaning often occurs quite suddenly. Skilled activity is like that, be it learning to read or riding a bike: suddenly you can do it – and you never lose the knack.

Audio Reading

This is a form of paired reading for children who like to feel they are independent and in control. You need a personal stereo with headphones. Record on it stories *just ahead* of the child's present level, i.e. one they might be able to read with a bit of support.

They read the actual story with the book in front of them but with your recorded voice of the same story coming through the headphones. They can turn the volume of this down so that it is little more than a background support. *Tell them to read the story rather than listen to your voice* – they'll still pick it up.

You'll need to judge how to pace the recording. What you are supporting is the beginning of *silent* reading (which is how skilled readers do it) and that is faster than normal speech – though the child won't be going very fast to begin with and will probably be 'saying' the words in their head or under their breath.

Scrambled Sentences

A scrambled sentence is one where the words are in the wrong order. For example:

my bus mum drives a big

Putting the words in the right order to read:

my mum drives a big bus

involves working out the meaning of the sentence.

This is quite tricky, so:

* don't make the sentence more than six words long

* don't give the child more than five to do at any one time

* don't scramble the words too much to begin with

* try to work in a bit of humour.

Make up an A4 sheet with the five scrambled sentences written out and a line underneath for the child to write out the words in the correct order. Leave them to it, but keep a watchful eye.

Stories and Reading for Meaning

Which Word?

This is a bit like The Gap Game, except that a choice of words is supplied – which makes it easier. For example:

> **When it skidded on the ice, the car**
> *crept/crashed/crawled* **into a wall.**

The child has to put a circle round the word that makes sense.

What makes it *harder* is the confusion factor: the first two letters of each word are the same. This makes them use *context* for meaning and word *inspection* for accuracy.

Make up an A4 sheet with four or five sentences and three words for each sentence with the same two beginning letters.

Scrambled Word Cards

This is a version of Scrambled Sentences where the words are written out on separate word cards and the child has to move them around to make a sensible sentence. It's both easier because they don't have to write the sentence out and more difficult because they can get themselves into a muddle.

- Give the child the word cards set out in a nonsense order.

- Don't make the sentence more than six words long.

- Tell them to think what the sentence starts with.

- Prompt them if they get frustrated by their attempts.

- Three or four of these Scrambled Sentences is enough on any one occasion.

Silly Sentences

Here all the words are in the right order but one of them doesn't make sense. For example:

> **Mum bought me a new witch for my birthday.**

What the child has to do is cross out the silly word and write in the correct one:

watch

Mum bought me a new ~~witch~~ for my birthday.

Make up sentences and pick words that:

- are a bit of a joke

- *look* or *sound* a bit like the correct word

- are the right *kind* of word (in the grammatical sense).

A few more examples:

I went slimming in the hotel pool.
My dad made a mice pudding.

This makes a good end-of-session activity. About eight to an A4 page is enough.

Make a Sentence

1   Make up an A4 sheet with three or four sentences like this:

There	are / will be	too many / not enough	boys / girls	in / on	this	class / bus / tent

2   Explain to the child that they have to pick one word/phrase from each box to make a sensible sentence, and write it underneath.

3   Whether they get it right or not, talk through the other possibilities (including the silly ones!).

years

Grabble

This is like Scrabble®, but here you're putting together words to make sentences rather than letters to make words. It's best played with just the two of you.

As with Scrabble, where there are often heated arguments, in Grabble there'll be some arguments about whether something is a sentence or whether one word can *grammatically* follow on from another word. And a lot is learned from this.

1   Make up about ten four- to six-word sentences.

2   Write them out on individual word cards, using a small letter for the first word in the sentence.

3   Make the cards all the same size.

4   Shuffle the cards and cut to see who deals (the one who cuts the longest word).

5   Give ten cards to each person.

6   The one who didn't deal puts down the first word of a sentence.

7   The other player lays down a second word for that sentence.

8   The other player then has the choice of putting a third word to *that* sentence or starting a sentence going *down*, using *either* of the first two words as a starting point. Like this:

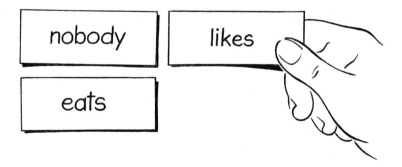

Stories and Reading for Meaning

9   The game develops from this point and might progress to look like this:

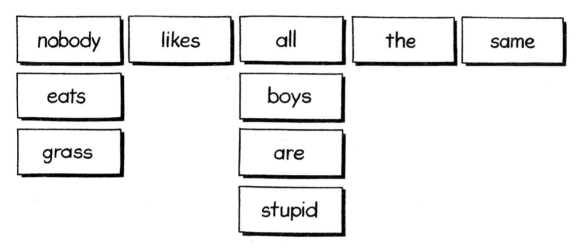

10   The rule for *down* and *across* sentences is that there has to be a gap between the sentences – for example: in the illustration, you could start a sentence down from 'same' or across from 'are'.

11   Anyone who can't go has to pick up another card.

12   The first player to get rid of all their cards wins the game.

Practising Reading Handwriting

This is an activity that helps children develop flexibility in the written/printed format of what they read.

You can do it informally by giving them someone's letter to read.

Or you can do it more systematically by getting two or three adults to copy out pages from a book of a suitable level and asking the child to read them (and what they think about the writing!). It's worth asking them to say exactly what it is about someone's handwriting that makes it easy (or difficult) to read, because that makes them think about it.

Children who can do this sort of thing easily have become skilled readers. No doubt about it.

READING HANDWRITING

When they are starting to read, children can only read words and letters when they are written in a standard way and big enough for them to see the differences between the letters. Variations like printers' *a* and *g* can throw them completely. Skilled readers don't even notice these variations.

In the same way, the skilled reader can cope with wild variations in spelling – some of them unique – and the even greater variety of handwriting styles. They pick out the 'distinctive features' of different letters even when they're written very differently.

It's partly a matter of practice – hence the Practising Reading Handwriting activity (on the previous page).

Timing Silent Reading

Speed is important in getting meaning from a book, because meaning goes beyond individual words, and if you go too slowly you can't hold enough words in your mind to get the proper sense of the sentence.

If children are reading silently, though, how do you know how well they're doing? You can get a pretty good idea just by watching them. But you can gauge their progress by *timing* them. Do it this way:

1   Ask them to start reading a page from a book when you say 'Now!' and to look up when they've reached the bottom of the page.

2   Start timing when you say 'Now!' and stop when they look up.

3   Work out their speed (words per minute) by estimating the

number of words on the page (multiply the number of words in a typical line by the number of lines), then dividing that by the total number of seconds they took and multiplying by sixty (easy on a calculator!). That gives you words per minute.

4   Q: How do you know they've read it?
     A: Ask them to tell you what happened.

5   Check their word recognition by pointing to some of the more difficult words on the page and asking what they are.

6   *Keep a record of the times*, and use the same book for retesting (on a different page).

Children find this an interesting thing to do and they can practise by timing themselves.

clock

car

pig

tree

PART II

Words

Word Books from Your Bookshop

Word books range from baby books, with only a small number of words in them, up to '1000 Word' books for children aged three to six. These are aimed mainly at developing the child's spoken language. But they also make children more *word-aware* – they come to see what written and printed words are about.

Some words have a special appeal for young children, even if they don't entirely understand them – like the word *soporific* in the opening sentence of Beatrix Potter's *The Tale of the Flopsy Bunnies*. This is often to do with how words sound: young children are very sensitive to the sounds that make up words, which is why they enjoy rhymes, and this skill helps them to become good readers. So focusing on printed words (how they *look*) and saying them (how they *sound*) is important right from the beginning.

Storybook Words

Children often start noticing individual words while sharing a storybook with an adult. When you're reading to them, sometimes point to the words one by one – but don't do it all the time, as it can make even adults read in a stilted manner.

Show the child that the gaps mark the beginning and end of words. Later, ask them to point to the words while you read them. With repeated reading of favourite stories children quite often start to recognize some words in the story without any prompting. These are usually especially interesting words, not necessarily 'easy' ones – like *dinosaur*, for example. Since this is quite an achievement for a young child, make a point of putting these special words in their Word Book (see the next page). This will also encourage the word-searching habit – looking out for words they can recognize. To begin with, children do this very slowly – rather in the way that they are slow in producing their earliest spoken words. Don't force the pace. Encourage them in the way that has been described but otherwise let nature take its course – as in learning to talk.

CAPITAL LETTERS AND SMALL LETTERS

Small or 'lower-case' letters are easier for young children to differentiate than capital or 'upper-case' letters because of the bits that stick up (ascenders) and the bits that hang down (descenders). So, when writing, always use small letters except for the first letters of proper names.

The Home-Made Word Book

A Home-Made Word Book is an excellent way of helping a child to build up a nucleus of words they can recognize. You need a ring binder with loose-leaf sheets, or a large scrapbook. Stick a picture on each page and write the word underneath.

Most of these words will be nouns, but there are some adjectives (especially 'how you feel' words like: *hot*, *happy*, *sad* and *sleepy*) that children like and which can be illustrated in some way. The words must be the child's own choice – so that it's *their* Word Book. The pictures can be a mixture of photographs (good for pets or members of the family, or anything that is difficult to draw), cut-outs from magazines, or drawings by the child or yourself. Write the words *big*, but use capitals only for the first letter of proper names because that never changes. Young children have difficulty in understanding that the word *dog*, for example, can also be written as *Dog* or *DOG*.

Children enjoy turning the pages, looking at the pictures and saying the words. To begin with, of course, they're just memorizing but they soon come to recognize some of the words without the picture. When you're quite sure of this, perhaps by covering up the pictures, you can test them by writing the words on Flash Cards and running through them with the child. Children love showing off their competence!

Although you should go through the book with them regularly, they will enjoy reading it for themselves and will do this without any encouragement from you.

Should we be encouraging 2-year-olds to read words?

Given half a chance, children will do it without any encouragement. Here's a personal anecdote.

At one time I was doing research on children's first sentences in speech. I regularly visited a group of children who were at the one-word stage. The mothers were keeping records of the first signs of their children putting words together.

One little girl was the star performer. At eighteen months she moved straight from single words to three-word sentences and accelerated from that point.

About three months later when I visited, her mother told me how they had been looking at a picture word book when they came to the page that said 'apple'. The little girl looked at this, got down from the sofa, went to the bookcase, found a cookery book her mother had been using, turned the pages and found a recipe with the word *apple* in the title.

No direct 'teaching' here. From around the age of two years, children often start to 'notice' words. Parents who respond to this are responding to something that is entirely natural. The roots of reading failure may lie in a lack of response to the interest that children spontaneously display.

Labelling Drawings

Young children produce a lot of drawings. At first these are quite simple 'one-object'-type drawings. These might be candidates for the Word Book – after all, if they're keen enough to *draw* something, they might want to read the word as well.

As they get a bit older children start to produce quite complex drawings of a 'panorama' type, with individual items well spaced out. You can use some of these to put small labels on the different objects or people in the pictures. And you can pin them up in the kitchen or the child's bedroom.

Don't expect the child to read the words, although the link between words and pictures may well start in this way. For the moment it is quite enough that they are getting the idea of the written word.

Which Word Shall I Write?

Children like to feel 'in control' of an adult. In this activity the child tells you a word they want you to write. It is best done on the floor with big sheets of paper and a broad marker pen in some lively colour. Size and colour contrast make the words more readable and the result more impressive. You simply ask what word they want you to write, doing this perhaps half a dozen times for different words. You can cut the words out to make very big Flash Cards and spread them around. Then ask: 'Which one says _____?' Since they've asked for the words in the first place, with a little help children can often pick them out.

The write style

For the first three years or so of school, before they learn 'joined-up' writing, children are taught to write letters separately.

The exact style can vary from one area of the country to another – you need to find out the way children are taught to write letters in the school your child is (or will be) attending. This may seem unimportant but children can get confused if they are taught one thing at home and another at school.

• Always use lower-case letters, except for the first letter of proper names.

• For a long time children will need a starting dot, usually at the top on the left or right, on an outline. To begin with, the outline should be big, bright and obvious. Gradually you can make it more and more unobtrusive until it's only a fine pencil line.

• It's also important to show the child the correct *direction* to go. If they get this wrong they will get into a muddle. For example:

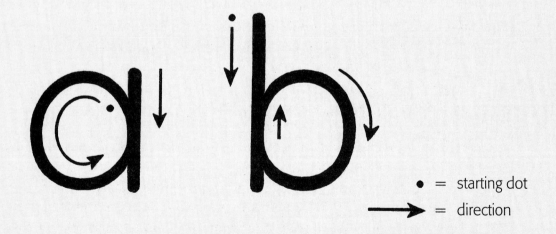

● = starting dot

———→ = direction

• You may need to guide the child's hand to start with. You do this by putting your fingers lightly on the back of their hand and steering them.

Little Words on Big Words

A variation and extension of the previous activity is to make up small Flash Cards of the same words and say: 'Let's put these little cards on the words that are the same.' Show the child how you hold the card you're matching against each one of the big cards in turn until you find the one that's the same. Then say: 'Now you do it!' and give the child one of the cards.

If they make a mistake, point out to them how the letters of the words are different, find the correct one and point to each letter in turn, saying: 'That's the same, that's the same . . .'

Matching may seem obvious to an adult, but to young children who haven't learned to notice the details of letters it's quite a demanding task. And if they learn to look at letters carefully they will learn to read more easily.

Labels Around the Home

Just labelling things and leaving it at that is unlikely to have any effect on a child: they need to be *involved*.

Ask the child to look for something and then give them the correct label to go with it. These need to be fairly big, on thin card and with a piece of Blu-Tack® at the back if they can't be propped up.

When they've labelled three or four objects, say, for example, 'Bring me the one that says *cushion*.' The real object, of course, tells the child what the word says, but it also focuses them on the word.

Logos

Point out to your child those international company signs that are not only a name but also a characteristic design (like Coca-Cola® or McDonald's). Once children get the idea, they will start searching for them and 'reading' the signs for themselves. These words and pictures can also be cut out of magazines and pasted in the Word Book – with the word written in ordinary lettering underneath the cut-out.

The Shopping List Game

Don't try this when you're in a rush or feeling hassled!

Make up a *real* shopping list for the child. Write on it the kind of things you can easily draw a simple picture for alongside the word. Tins and packages aren't much good (they all look the same), eggs and bottles are too risky, so it usually works best with fruit and vegetables (especially if you colour the drawings). Let them have responsibility for the things on their list.

Supermarkets that provide special mini-trolleys are ideal – provided you supervise...

Tracing Over Words

Some children find this frustratingly difficult for a long time; others make rapid progress. It doesn't seem to have much to do with the child's age or intelligence. Don't persist if it causes problems.

Make a simple drawing and then write the name underneath in highlighter pen or something similar you can write over. Give the child a black felt-tip pen, mark a 'starting dot' for each letter and then guide them as they trace each letter.

When they've reached the point where they're satisfied with the result, you can let them trace over words in their Word Book.

HOLDING A PENCIL

What are usually called 'motor' skills develop at different rates in different children – and may not keep pace with their language or intellectual development.

The American psychologist, Simon Krippner, in an article entitled 'The Boy Who Read at 18 Months' and whom Krippner saw when the child was four years old, reported that 'Larry Wilson failed a reading readiness test but read material at the second and third grade level [i.e. 8- to 10-year level] . . . He could barely hold a pencil but knew the letters of the alphabet.'

Difficulties in holding a pencil (a *fine* motor skill) cause children a lot of frustration. Thick, stubby crayons are easier to hold but don't give very satisfactory results. The best thing is to put an extra grip on a pencil. In educational stationers you can buy slide-on rubber grips, but sticking plaster (the rough, not the smooth, kind) wrapped round the pencil works just as well.

Matching Labels

1   Cut out labels (just the *words*) from a selection of household goods.

2   You need *two* sets, of between six and ten items.

3   Lay out one set on the table, hold the other set in your hand.

4   Give your child one of the labels and ask them to bring you the one that matches.

5   When they do this, *tell* them what the label says.

6   After a couple of practices, ask your child to tell you what the label says.

This is halfway to true word recognition – they'll still be getting something from the design and colour of the packet.

Copying Under Words

From an adult point of view there may seem little difference between tracing over words and copying underneath them. But for young children it is a big step forward. Even when they can trace over perfectly well, children may be completely at sea when it comes to copying without any supports (apart from seeing what they have to copy).

You can still give them a starting dot and guide them with your fingers. Talk them through it as well ('down . . . and round').

Again, when they can achieve a result they're pleased with they can copy under the words in their Word Book – or anything else that you've labelled for them.

years

WASN'T THIS SUPPOSED TO BE A BOOK ABOUT READING, NOT WRITING?

Correct. But early writing activities, like tracing and copying letters and words, are an important part of learning to read because they make children *look* at the letters very carefully. Reading depends on the child noticing *very small differences* between letters. That takes time.

Writing Their Own Name

Independent writing (without a copy) is not something usually achieved in preschool. In its early stages writing comes very slowly indeed. But being able to write your own name has a special significance, justifies the effort, and is always *highly* satisfactory to young children.

The progression is straightforward:

1   tracing over the word,

2   copying underneath it, and

3   writing it without a copy (the biggest leap of all).

This last stage is the troublesome one. The way you do it is to write the child's name on a card, put it at the top of a sheet of paper, tell them to look at it hard, turn the card over and write their name. Then they can turn the card back and check.

Many children will want to do this by themselves (because it's self-checking), without any adult interference . . .

Don't push this preschool, but some children will want to learn to write other words – see the suggestions on page 63. If they're happy to do it, then let them.

Big Words, Little Words

Small children often don't understand that a word that is longer to say will *look* longer on the page. They may think it works quite differently, i.e. that bigger *things* make a bigger *word*. Ask the child to tell you big words and little words, for you to write down and for them to sort into two piles. If they get it wrong, hold up the card and say: 'Is that a big [or little] word?'

Children like this activity because they feel they've got the adult working for them!

Read-a-Word

When you're sharing a storybook you can give the child a few words to read in it; these can be marked with a highlighter pen. Don't pick too many – one a page is plenty – and choose words where the sense of the sentence 'points' to the word, e.g. 'Our baby has two teeth and he *bites*.'

If the child hesitates, prompt them with the sound of the first two letters of the word. If that isn't enough, say the word for them. Don't let the activity get in the way of the story.

LEFT HAND, RIGHT HAND

From about the age of eighteen months children start to show a clear preference for using one hand more than the other for 'fine control' activities: scribbling, picking up small objects, using a fork or spoon, hammering, screwing and unscrewing, and so on. Around eight per cent of boys and six per cent of girls show a consistent left preference; usually this is an inherited tendency. But, to begin with, many children are not so consistent. In this case it is better to encourage the use of the right hand provided the child doesn't resist. 'Encourage' means no more than putting a spoon or crayon in their right hand.

REVERSALS AND MIRROR-WRITING

Young children often reverse letters when they're reading and when they start to write (especially *b*, *d* and *s*). They even reverse whole words that make sense both ways (like *was* and *saw*). This is so common as to be normal and remains common until the age of seven or eight. It does not mean the child is 'dyslexic'. Mirror-writing is less common, but appears to be 'normal' for left-handed children (because it is more 'natural' to write outwards from your body-line). They soon learn the 'correct' direction.

Matching Words to Words Under Pictures

This is an intermediate stage between matching words to words and matching words to pictures.

1   You have a set of pictures with the words written underneath – four or five set out in a row.

2   You have separate cards (a different colour helps) with the same words on them. To make it a bit more challenging, you can have two or three additional cards with words that don't match on them.

3   The challenge is to match the cards that just have words on them to the word/picture cards. This helps to establish the link between word and picture.

Do this for twenty to thirty words and then move on, using the same pictures, to straightforward word–picture matching (see p. 66). You'll find that this preliminary stage gives the child a better chance of success.

Words Across the Room

Here you make up *giant* word cards from the Word Book or a very familiar storybook. They need to be really big – at least A4-size – and coloured card is best.

You prop the cards up on the sofa – three or four at a time – and then, seating yourself on the other side of the room with the child, say: 'Bring me the word that says _____'.

Hold the child so that they look at all the words before darting across the room. The *size* of the word cards makes them more 'visible' and the activity dimension adds to the fun.

The same idea is used in the 'giant' books that are now so popular. Although designed for use by teachers reading a story to a group of children, they have immense appeal to individual children, and some public libraries stock them.

IDENTIFYING WORDS AND RECOGNIZING WORDS

These are quite different things and one is much easier than the other – and leads on to it. When you ask children to *identify* words you spread out the word cards and say, for example: 'Which one says *cheese*?' Here they've got the visual word and the spoken word – they just have to put the two together.

When you ask them to recognize a word, you show them the word card and ask: 'What does that say?' All they have to go on is the visual word – the rest has to come out of their head.

Words that a child has difficulty recognizing should be dealt with at the 'identification' level. Once they can do this easily they are not far off being able to recognize them.

Posting Words

This is a way of matching words to picture-words, (and, later on, words to pictures) that appeals to young children. Make a posting box out of an old shoebox and cover it with wallpaper or coloured wrapping paper. Make a posting slit towards the top.

Use the set of picture-word cards from the activity on page 60. Put one of the picture-word cards underneath the posting slot and ask the child to post the matching word in the slot. Later on you can use this as an alternative to the straightforward picture – word matching on page 66.

Playing Shopping

1   Set out half a dozen household commodities on the table (tea, soap, salt, etc.).

2   Make up Flash Cards with the words on.

3   Give them one card at a time and say: 'This word says _____. You bring me the _____.'

4   After a couple of runs of this, give them the card and say: 'Bring me this one.'

WHY WORD RECOGNITION IS IMPORTANT

Phonics (sounding out the letters of a word) is part of learning to read, but this is not how skilled readers operate. They recognize words visually at high speed (300–400 a minute is quite common). The value of phonics may be that it makes children look at words more carefully so that, at high speed, they pick up the small differences between the letters.

My Name is _____
Happy Birthday from _____

Children who are very keen to go a bit further when they can write their name can go on to write:

My name is _____

- To begin with, let them write in their name and trace over the other words.

- Then let them copy all the words underneath.

- When you feel they are ready, get them to look at the sentence, turn it over, write from memory, turn it back again and check what they have written.

Another extension of using their name is for the child to make birthday cards for people (stick-on shapes work well, especially the glittery ones) and then learn to write:

Happy Birthday from _____

inside – following the sequence from tracing to copying to writing from memory.

Learning to write both these simple phrases gives practice with most of the different basic letter shapes.

Words

THE SEX DIFFERENCE

Boys are much more likely than girls to have reading difficulties. Usually these are not due to any profound problems; boys often just seem less interested in reading. But they are storing up trouble for themselves in the future.

Right from the start girls have a language advantage. They are usually talking earlier, make faster progress and have fewer speech disorders. Early difficulties and delay in spoken language are linked to later reading difficulties. The better-than-average performance of girls at secondary school seems to be due partly to their superior literacy. But their attitude to school work is a major factor as well.

Interestingly, *precocious* readers (those who are reading before the age of three or four) are more likely to be boys. And when girls *do* have reading problems they are often very severe.

Matching Words to Pictures with the First Letter Showing

This is a halfway house to straightforward matching of words to pictures – a more difficult task.

Here the pictures have the *first letter* of the word underneath them, which gives the child a clue. But, so as not to make it *too* simple, you have *six* pictures in pairs that begin with the same letter (*ball, baby; dog, door; tree, table*), and six corresponding word cards.

The child has to work out what letter the word begins with. They then have a choice of two words beginning with that letter to make the correct match. Quite difficult enough at this stage!

Words

Find Me . . .

Make up five or six word cards for things around the house that can easily (and safely) be brought to you by the child.

Start by making sure they can *identify* the words (see p. 61). Then, handing them one card at a time, say: 'Find me this' (but don't say the word). Whatever they have to look for should not be in sight (but, at the same time, not so difficult to find that they get fed up).

VISUAL DYSLEXIA

Skilled reading is visual: skilled readers get the meaning from rapid visual checking of the words on the page. *Visual dyslexics* can't do this: their reading is inaccurate and slow and their spelling is worse. Spelling often remains weak even after they have learned to read.

Visual dyslexics compensate by using their phonic knowledge, and the main teaching methods (as in Beve Hornsby and Frula Shear's *Alpha to Omega* programme – see p. 126) are systematic phonics programmes. There are disadvantages to this (phonics is not the complete answer) and it is certainly laborious, but there is little alternative.

Most children spell phonetically to begin with and are very skilful at it (a boy I was testing once wrote down the name of his school as 'Hinkle Gooney' – for 'Hinckley Junior') but they gradually learn to spell visually – which is what skilled spellers do. Those who persist with spelling-as-it-sounds after the age of eight or nine need some extra help. But remember: we all spell phonetically if we've never seen the word.

Matching Words to Pictures

This is the beginning of true word recognition – recognizing the words that go with pictures.

To begin with, use words and pictures they already know from their Word Book. Three or four words and the corresponding pictures are enough for a start.

Set the pictures out in a row, take the word cards and say: 'We're going to put these words under the right pictures. This is a picture of a pig. Now which word says *pig*?' Do the first one yourself and then give the child a word card to see how they manage. This gets easier, of course, as there are fewer pictures and word cards left – but there's no harm in that.

Once the child can do this fairly easily, you can make it more demanding in two ways:

- by increasing the number of cards (although six to eight is probably enough)

- by introducing words the child doesn't know so well, and one or two they don't know at all. If they tackle these last, they'll usually get them right because there are fewer choices to make.

Turnover Cards

Children like this game because it's one they can do without any help (= interference) from adults at all.

Turnover cards have a picture on one side and the word on the other. Include a few words they know, some they're not sure about, and a couple they don't know at all.

You can make up as many cards as you like, but a set of ten is probably enough for a child at any one time.

The child lays the cards out picture side down, tries to read each word and turns over the card to check. This self-checking is what appeals to children because if they can't read the word, or get it wrong, nobody knows about it except themselves.

Once they've mastered the words (or most of them) they can bring them to you to demonstrate their success.

Picture–Word Matching (Self-Checking)

This is like a combination of Picture–Word Matching and Turnover Cards (see opposite).

The basic task is to match word cards to pictures, *but* on the other side of the word card is the picture that has to be matched so that the child can *check* whether they've made the right match by turning over the card. The pictures have to be identical – easy with a photocopier.

Labelling Round the Room

Here the word cards are matched to real objects.

Make up five or six Flash Cards (with a bit of Blu-Tack at the back if necessary) for as many objects around the room you're working in. Lay the words out on the floor or a coffee table.

Start out by saying, for example: 'Which one says *computer*?' If the child makes the right choice, say: 'Right. Now stick the word on the computer.' And so on.

When they can do this easily with prompting, say: 'Now I'm not going to give you any help.' Hand them the word cards one by one and say: 'Where does this go?'

Children enjoy the physical activity involved in this game – but they're still learning something!

SHOULDN'T TEACHERS BE DOING ALL THIS?

The answer is that it's impossible. There are around five class-time hours in a teacher's day. A class is likely to have nearly thirty children in it (and sometimes more). The full curriculum has to be fitted into that time slot for all these children. It is quite impossible to give much individual teaching time to children even when they need it. But individual teaching is by far the most effective. In general it is only parents who can provide that.

The Pictogram Game

A pictogram is a simple picture that tells you what a word is or replaces a word.

You write a very simple story on one sheet of A4, thinking about the nouns you can easily do a pictogram for. For example:

The little [girl] climbed a [tree] to look for her [cat]

and so on.

Because nouns carry maximum meaning, they help the child to read the in-between words.

The next stage is to make the pictograms smaller and put the nouns in underneath them. Nouns (and verbs) are usually the 'new' element in a book the child hasn't read before. The other words are mostly common to *all* books (see list on p. 75).

Highlight Matching

One variation of matching words to pictures is to write a short list of words under each picture and ask the child to highlight the correct one.

You can make this easier or more difficult by:

- altering the number of words (from two to five is enough)

- making the words more or less difficult, i.e. the most difficult would be five words, all the same length, and all beginning with the same letter.

Word–Picture Slide-Matching

This involves spending the money to buy slide film and mounts but can be well worth it.

It works particularly well with children who find Picture–Word Matching (see p. 66) difficult or not exciting enough.

You need:

- an automatic camera with flash
  (which means most modern cameras)

- slide film

- slide mounts

- slide viewer.

Film processors can mount your slides for you but it is unnecessary and expensive. With a box of plastic mounts and a pair of scissors you can easily make your own.

Having decided on the words, you take colour slides of the people, animals or objects. *Get close in* – otherwise you'll have a small object in a lot of space.

Using half a dozen slides at a time, set the word cards out in front of the child. Put the slide viewer on a book: this gives a little platform in front. Drop a slide in the viewer and say: 'Put the word that says _____ here.' The child then presses the slide down to light up – and checks whether they've made the right choice.

Word Bingo

This is a word-matching and recognition game you play with the child, who has as good a chance of winning as you have. If other members of the family can be persuaded to play, so much the better.

1   Make up four or more bingo cards with six words on each – there can be some overlap between different cards.

2   Then make individual word cards and lay them face down in a pile. The words should come from the Word Book or other source familiar to the child.

3   Each player picks up a card in turn. If it matches a word on their card, they cover it. If it doesn't, they put it back at the bottom of the pile.

4   The first player to get a full house wins the game (provide a prize!).

Words

Peg Letters

1 Make a 'clothes line' between two heavy pieces of furniture, and collect some pegs together.

2 Make up some letter cards of a good size and on bright card, with a fold at the top so they can be pegged on the line. Include all the vowels and all the consonants except *q*, *x*, *y* and *z*.

3 Show the child how you can make up three-letter words ('vowel in the middle') – such as *hug*, *rug*, *fat*, *mat*, etc.

4 Do it in turn, with you making a word, then the child.

Even very young children will happily do this because of the activity element.

Read and Draw (Words)

All children like drawing. Here they have to read a word in order to know what to draw.

1 Draw lines to divide an A4 sheet in four.

2 At the top of each box write the word that tells them what they have to draw (*snake*, *dog*, *baby*, and so on).

3 Explain to the child that they have to read the word and then draw what it says.

Flash Cards

These are a teaching 'basic' for word recognition – individual cards of words a child *needs* to know and which you show them more and more quickly until they can recognize them 'in a flash'.

There is a big difference between words that children can recognize when they think about it and those that they can recognize immediately.

Reading is about recognizing words very quickly indeed so

that you get directly to the meaning. *Some Flash-Card practice should be part of every session.*

These are the main sources for finding the words to teach:

* the child's present reading-scheme book: pick out nouns, adjectives and verbs from here (these are usually specific to the story)

* the list of 100 'high-frequency' words on page 75; these form the major part of *all* books: they're not very exciting or easy to remember, which is why children need some help with them

* their Word Book

* any other favourites for rereading at home

* words connected with their special interests – whether reading is involved or not.

When you've got your word lists, where do you start?

1   Make up test cards with about twenty words on each; you'll probably need two or three of these to begin with.

2   Run through them quickly with the child, making a note of the words in these categories:

   a *words they can read right away (discard those)*   **(✓✓)**
   b *words they can read when they think about it*   **(✓)**
   c *near misses: not quite right*   **(O)**
   d *words they get completely wrong or don't attempt.*   **(✗)**

3   Put together about twenty to thirty words from *b*, *c* and *d*, always including some from each. Focus on about half a dozen words in any one session.

4   Move on after about two weeks to another batch.

5   Don't carry on adding words for too long: once they've learned about 150–200 in this way, concentrate on some of the later activities – *aids* to word recognition such as phonic and comprehension skills. However, continue to practise words that they have special difficulty in remembering.

Making a Word Wall

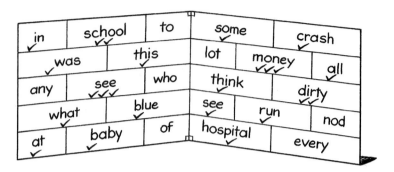

Children need *visible* evidence of progress (as we all do!). A Word Wall is a good way of testing progress and showing the child what they've achieved.

Make a Word Wall by taping two A4 sheets of card together (parcel tape is best). Divide the pages up into brick-like rectangles; stagger them like brickwork. You write all the words on the wall – one on each brick.

Test the half-dozen or so words you are teaching on Flash Cards at the *beginning* and *end* of each session. Tick those the child gets right. Three ticks and a word counts as learned. Then the child colours the brick in.

At any one time, work from a group of twenty to thirty words (not all in the same activity – half a dozen is usually enough). Make a new Word Wall every couple of weeks. Any words not learned by then go on to the next one.

*S*imon is in his first year at primary school and is very keen to learn the words which he brings home in a tin, and to practise his school 'reader'. He won't accept activities that are too 'game-like'. He sees school reading as being proper work and is prepared to sit at it. The youngest in his large family, his elder sister helps him.

A typical session for him might include:

• Flash-Card practice using the Word Wall (as above)

• practising First-Letter Sounds using pictures from magazines (p. 108)

• hearing him read his school reader (p. 28).

The Sentence Maker

Learning words from Flash Cards is a big achievement to begin with and it continues to be important for those words that are troublesome to remember. But there comes a point where the activity starts to pall. After all, what do you *do* with these words? A Sentence Maker is a way of putting words to use by making up sentences.

Writing complete sentences just out of your head is quite a difficult task for young children. However, if they have the words they know on cards, they can put together a sentence from these (usually with adult help). They can then read the sentence and copy it out.

You need to make sure they know the 'link' words that join up the nouns and verbs and adjectives (see the list on p. 75). Some extra Flash-Card practice may be necessary here.

Make a folder that the child can keep their *small* word cards in. The folder is made from two A4 sheets of card, hinged with parcel tape. Cut strips of card going across the page, and stick these with adhesive tape. Finally make up small individual cards of the words the child has learned through Flash-Card practice or in their Word Book, *together with* some of the common 'link' words such as *and*, *on*, *in*, *of*, etc.

Show them how you can pick words out to make a sentence, setting these out in a writing/drawing book and then copying the sentence underneath. To begin with, keep the sentences short (four or five words). Some children get the hang of this very quickly; others need more help and encouragement. Important for the child is that it is something they can do *without* adult help eventually.

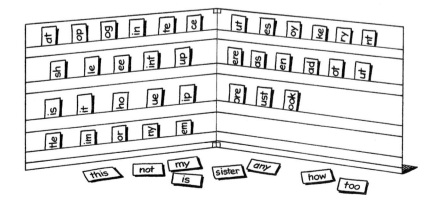

Action Words: Can You Do This?

This is an excellent way of encouraging children to recognize words *quickly*. Because it is a very *physical* activity, young children enjoy it very much. It's a bit like The Instruction Game (p. 36).

1   Make up a set of cards, with an action word on each:

sit	**laugh**	**stand**	**clap**
jump	**kneel**	**smile**	**point**

and so on.

2   To begin with, put a stick man or a face or hand drawing next to the word. Ask: 'Can you do this?'

3   After one or two sessions just show the child the word on its own. As they get better, speed up.

How Many Words Can You Make?

This is a good end-of-session activity, which encourages children to be flexible and analytic about words.

1   Make up an A4 sheet with four consonants and two vowels at the top. For example:

t   e   g   w   m   a

2   Put about five boxes below to write the words in.

3   Ask the child: 'See how many three-letter words you can make from these letters. Let's do the first one together.'

4   Show how you have to play around with the possibilities: 'Is there such a thing as a *weg*?'

100 high-frequency words

in	of	here	this
it	so	no	before
and	they	if	who
had	his	you	soon
not	old	more	girl
on	me	some	he
but	she	when	to
can	an	where	you
get	by	am	as
will	out	I	we
did	them	that	all
just	only	for	do
went	little	said	her
big	their	one	now
from	about	him	down
look	what	up	our
then	every	my	were
see	sat	has	come
which	is	or	over
ask	the	go	much
yes	are	into	right
got	have	there	want
boy	with	been	any
was	at	of	very
a	be	like	give

Kim's Game

This is a variant of a game we all know. It provides excellent memory training and speeds up word recognition.

Set out six Flash Cards of words the child can recognize. Say: 'I'm going to let you look at these while I count to ten, then I want you to tell me how many you can remember.'

Spot the Difference

This activity helps children to look for differences between words that are the same *length* and have almost the same letters – a problem with many common words. Children can do this quite quickly (good for an end-of-session activity), but it is excellent training none the less.

1   On an A4 sheet put ten to fifteen of these 'confuseable' words down the left-hand side. Choose common words with three to five letters in them.

2   Then separate them off from the rest of the page by drawing a line down and write what *looks* like the same word three times on the same line across, *except that* one of the words is one letter different.

3   The child has to underline the word that's different and put a ring around the letter that's different from the other words. Vary the position of the 'rogue' word.

Here are some confuseable word pairs (you'll easily think of others):

top/tip, hot/hit, sat/sit, hot/hat, fit/fat
and so on

hard/hand, thin/this, fine/fire, rope/ripe
and so on

chair/chain, strip/strap, shoot/shout, sleep/sheep, horse/house
and so on.

Fast-Track

There is a big difference between recognizing words quickly and recognizing them slowly: it's a different kind of skill. *Skilled reading means recognizing words very fast indeed.*

This activity is one you do only when the child has a good sight vocabulary – words they can get right on Flash Cards. You don't use words they're not sure about.

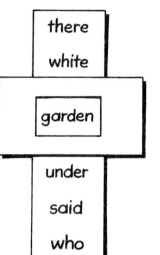

1   Pick ten to fifteen words the child can definitely recognize.

2   Make up a word window as shown. Write the words on a long strip of card that you pull through a 'window' that shows only one word at a time.

3   Say: 'You know all these words. But let's see how fast you can say them.'

4   Run through them, allowing about two seconds at first (one – pause – two – pause – move on).

5   If that's successful try it at the one-second rate (one – pause – move on). And then even faster (one, move on).

Because they *know* the words, children don't feel threatened by this and it does speed up their word recognition.

Make a Dictionary

When your child can *definitely* read a word they can put it in their personal dictionary.

Buy a small 'alphabetical' notebook and ask them to make a decorative dictionary cover, and encourage them to use their dictionary when they're doing any writing.

Children learn a lot from this, incidentally – not least how to *use* a dictionary. You can take this further by showing them how, in a real dictionary, you have to go past the first letter because the second letters of the words are also in alphabetical order. You can show them how this works with a telephone directory as well – good practical skills.

Jumbled Letters

This activity is not as simple as it seems because, for the child, what's there on the page is rather distracting. For example:

pli

What word is that? Children have to reorder the letters in their minds until they come up with the one that makes sense:

lip

Make up a list of five to ten three-letter words where the letters are jumbled up, with answer boxes next to them. For example:

guj	☐		**pir**	☐
rac	☐		**tne**	☐
pni	☐		**nsu**	☐

Ask the child to write the letters in the box in the correct order to make a word.

Children can be very slow with this at first, but once they get the idea they speed up. The value is that it makes them 'analytical' about the composition of words.

Speed Trials

This is another way to improve a child's speed of word recognition. The timing element makes it more fun. A stopwatch is ideal but an ordinary watch with a second hand or a kitchen timer does almost as well.

Children are not threatened by this because they already know they know the words, and they have to improve on their own best time – they're not competing with anyone else. Because this is quick and non-threatening, it makes a good end-of-session activity.

1   Make up a set of ten words they know.

2   Show the cards one by one: three seconds each to begin with (one – pause – two – pause – three – pause – down).

3   If they get them all right, go on to a two-second exposure (one – pause – two – pause – down).

4   Then move on to a one-second exposure (one – pause – down).

5   If that works, go for a half-second exposure (one, down).

6   After each run-through, the child writes down their time. If they make a mistake you don't count the time and you give them another go at the same exposure. Then move on.

The Spelling Way to Read Words

Some words, often very common words like those in the list on page 75, can cause children persistent problems – almost as if they have a *blind spot*. These need to be *over-learned* using a spelling technique called the LOOK–COVER–WRITE–CHECK technique. It is simple, self-checking and very effective. In most cases, it is all that is needed.

You need to write three or four of these problem words on a card and tell the child:

* to LOOK hard at the words and try to remember how they LOOK

* to COVER the card or turn it over

* to WRITE the words *quickly* and without 'thinking' about them

* to uncover the card and CHECK.

This is repeated until the words are spelt correctly. The visual-memory training involved usually enables them to read the word(s) on sight in the future.

Word endings

Accurate word recognition means paying attention to how words end as well as how they begin. The endings shown here are particularly important because they don't sound as they look. Most of them have silent letters: children need to know this. Here's a list (activities follow):

You don't sound the *e*	*le*	as in	hand*le*
	el	as in	parc*el*
	ed	as in	kick*ed*
You don't sound the *o*	*our*	as in	col*our*
You don't sound the *a*	*ar*	as in	calend*ar*
They all say *shun*	*shion*	as in	cu*shion*
(or very nearly!)	*sion*	as in	televi*sion*
	tion	as in	sta*tion*
Soft *c*: you don't sound the *e*	*ce*	as in	dan*ce*
You don't sound the *o*	*ous*	as in	fam*ous*
You only sound the *t*	*ght*	as in	ni*ght*
You don't sound it at all	*gh*	as in	si*gh*
A special case!	*ough*	see page 122	

Highlight Silent Endings

1   Explain which letters you don't sound in the word endings in the box opposite.

2   Make up a list of twenty words with these endings – mixed up.

3   Ask the child to highlight the silent letters in these word endings.

    Choose from the following:

ght	might, night, fight, sight, tight, right, caught, taught
gh	sigh, high, thigh
el	kennel, tunnel, panel, flannel, parcel, cancel, novel, travel
ous	dangerous, glamorous, precious, gorgeous, famous
our	flavour, labour, glamour, harbour, favour, humour, colour
ed	kicked, rubbed, filled, cleaned, cracked, chopped, pinned (*trick ones*: patted, wetted, blotted)
ce	chance, dance, France, mince
le	bottle, kettle, table, stable, apple, handle, battle, uncle, puzzle, rattle, muscle.

Pick Your Ending

1   Make up an A4 sheet with these endings at the top:

ght gh el ous our ed ce le

2   Pick ten words from the list in Highlight Silent Endings (above) and set them out, missing off the ending, like this:

danger_____

3   Tell the child they have to pick the right ending from the list at the top and write it in. Sometimes more than one ending will fit.

Word-Slicing

'Big words' can be so offputting to children that they don't even look at them. In fact, it is often 'small' words that are harder to read.

BIG WORDS ARE MADE UP OF SMALL 'WORDS' THAT ARE EASY TO READ. Not all syllables are words, of course, but they are word-like.

What children have to learn is how to break big words up into syllables. The basic rules (for you to bear in mind) are given in the box opposite. Children need a lot of practice in this skill.

Start by taking an obviously *long* and *hard* word like *prehistoric*. Say: 'I'm going to show you how to read this word.' Put the first slice down and ask, 'What does that say?', then the next one, and so on. For example,

pre / his / tor / ic

or it could be

pre / his / to / ric

It doesn't really matter.

Go on to do this with five or six other words. Include this as one element in teaching sessions over a week. Increasingly ask the child to put the slices in. When you are sure they've got the idea, you can move on to the next activity.

Syllable-Slicing: Two, Three and Four

Once you feel that your child has the 'syllable idea', you can move on to this.

1   Starting with two-syllable words only, make up an A4 sheet set out like this:

empty   **prison**

| emp | ty | | |

and so on.

2   Explain to the child that each of the words has two syllables and that they have to write the separate syllables in the two boxes underneath.

3   Help them if they get into difficulties, reminding them of the rules – the most important of which is that each syllable has to have a vowel (or vowel equivalent like *y*) in it.

4   Ask them to read the word once they've sliced it.

Move on to three and then four syllables once two-syllable words become too easy.

Syllable-slicing: the rules

• A syllable has to sound like a word but it doesn't have to be a proper word:

op / po / site

• A syllable has to have at least one vowel in it (*a, e, i, o, u, y*):

in / ter / est

• Sometimes a vowel is a syllable on its own:

e / lec / tric

• When there are two consonants together, the break usually comes in the middle:

but / ter

except when they make a special sound together:

fa / ther   **fat / head**

one sound   separate sounds

• With a vowel followed by a consonant, the break usually comes before the consonant:

stu / pid   **cle / ver**

Words

Make Your Own Words

This is another way of approaching syllables and it really makes children think how words are made up.

1   Make up syllable cards as follows:

in	slow	vide	ex	out
ly	sent	do	tend	ing
pect	un	er	side	pro
safe	tect	be	pre	jump

All of these can be used to make up two-syllable words. Word beginnings are in rectangles; word endings are in ovals.

2   Show the child how to make up a word and ask them to write it down. This records their achievement.

3   Help them if they get into a muddle.

How Many Slices?

This is a tricky one, because the child has to do the syllable-slicing entirely in their head. A child who can do this easily has definitely got the idea.

1   Make up an A4 sheet as follows:

shower ☐	video ☐	upset ☐	amazing ☐
television ☐	washing ☐	breakfast ☐	pillow ☐
excavation ☐	stereo ☐	presently ☐	underground ☐

Words

2   Show the child how you say the word slowly so that you can *hear* the break between the syllables.

3   The child has to put the *number* of syllables in the box under the word.

4   Do the first one for them, then ask them to do the next one out loud while you watch and listen.

5   If they seem happy to continue on their own, leave them to it, but keep a watchful eye.

If it works well, repeat the activity – this time using words from the list below.

Useful words for syllable-slicing

Two syllables

carpet   broken   stupid   clever   inside   mistake   traffic
brother   sister   moment   parking   foolish   dislike
forward   expect   window   winter   chimney   lightning

Three syllables

important   disappear   exciting   separate   parachute   enormous
expected   fantastic   amazing   violent   photograph   atmosphere

Four syllables

intelligent   television   unimportant   unexpected
ridiculous   electronic   expedition   operation   accidental

8 ▶
years

Crosswords

This is quite a difficult game and it makes children think very carefully about how words are made up. Two or more people can play but it's quite complicated enough with two!

1   In the centre of an A4 sheet (lengthways) the first player (you!) writes out one long word of at least eight letters – like *elephant*.

2   The other player then has to make a word that uses one of the letters
    • as a beginning letter (*e*gg)
    • as a final letter (bal*l*)
    • as a middle letter (ha*n*d).
    Like this:

```
        b
        a               h
        l               a
    e l e p h a n t
        g               d
        g
```

Help with the spelling!

3   When there are up and down words, you can make words that go across. Like this:

```
        b
        a               h e a d
        l               a     i
    e l e p h a n t      n
        g               d     n
      p i g                    e
                               r
```

and so on.

4   Each letter in a word scores one. The first person to score fifty wins.

How Many Words?

This familiar activity is another excellent way of getting children to look and think about how words are made up – reading is a lot to do with a quick analytic approach to words.

You've played it yourself. You take a fairly long word, with a good mixture of letters, and see how many words you can make up from it.

It's a game a child will want to play on their own (showing you the result).

Here's a list of words that work well:

tomatoes	**accident**
umbrella	**ambulance**
explosion	**adventure**
disappear	**parachute**
underneath	**enormous**

Give the child a couple of words on any one occasion. If they enjoy it, you will easily think of other suitable words.

PART III

Sounds and Letters

Sharing Rhymes

There is something so compelling about the sound of traditional nursery rhymes that even babies respond to them, especially if they are sung. It doesn't matter that they don't understand the words. When they're a little older you can introduce the child to rhymes involving actions, like 'Ride a Cock Horse' or 'Pat-a-Cake'.

Books with nursery rhymes should come in early and may appeal before the child is ready for storybooks. Saying or singing rhymes together paves the way for reading stories together later on.

Recording Rhymes

When your child can say or sing a rhyme confidently, try tape-recording them. This encourages the child to listen more carefully and, in particular, to listen to themselves – a kind of feedback they can get in no other way.

Finishing Off

Start with familiar rhymes, leaving a space for the child to fill in the rhyming word ('Baa, baa, black sheep, have you any wool? Yes sir, yes sir, three bags *full!*'). When they're adept at this you can move on to making up rhyming couplets where the sense is obvious (This is the cat that lives in our house. Look what he's caught: a little brown *mouse.*')

LISTENING TO LEARN

Children learning to talk are acute listeners: they have to be. They are picking up exactly the accent of the adults around them. To achieve this, children have to be highly sensitive to how words sound. We can use this sensitivity to help them learn to read, encouraging them to identify the sounds that make up words.

What Goes . . .?

For young children, getting the idea that objects or animals make a distinctive sound seems to help them understand that letters also make their own sound. It also helps them to *listen* more carefully and work out how to make the sounds themselves.

Pictures of animals work best and you can easily find these in book form. With two or more to choose from you ask, for example, 'Which one goes "miaow"?' If the child doesn't respond right away, point to the picture and say: 'The *pussycat* goes "miaow". How does it go?'

When the child can do that confidently, you point to the other pictures, one at a time, and ask: 'How does this one go?'

The next step is to do without pictures and ask: 'Tell me what goes "baa"?', and the child has to give you the name of the animal.

Alphabet Books

Alphabet books include some of the best books published for children and they will appeal to those so young that the alphabet itself only gradually takes their attention. If you can find one that attracts your child it will be a constant companion, and a lot will be learned from it. The most useful kind is where both the letters (upper and lower case) and the sounds are highlighted.

Try borrowing some from the library to see if there is a particular book that takes the child's fancy. Bookshops will have a selection of the most recently published ones, but not necessarily the old favourites (though these can sometimes be ordered).

Clapping Rhymes

Some rhymes are good for singing and clapping (like 'Pat-a-Cake'), because of the way they break the syllables up.

This is *the* best way to start children noticing syllable patterns because (without being aware of it) they will learn where the breaks come and also which syllables are emphasized – the rhythm. More subtly, they will also notice the sounds that make up the syllables.

Find a Rhyme

Some children get the idea of what a rhyme is quite easily. Practice with nursery rhymes builds up to that. Other children find it much more difficult and seem to have a 'blind spot'. If that's the case, don't battle away at it.

Say, for example, 'Tell me a word that rhymes with *mat*.' If you don't get an immediate response, say: 'Well, *cat* rhymes with *mat*.' Can you think of another one?' Use three-letter words to make it easy; if this becomes too easy, move on to longer words: *head/said, jumping/bumping, cook/book*, etc.

Rhymes don't just involve listening for the *ends* of words; they go further back into the word than that. And in this activity the child also has to distinguish the beginning of the word (in order to come up with a different one that rhymes).

Odd One Out

Say about four words – for example, *tin, bin, cup, pin* – and ask the child which one doesn't rhyme. Use only three-letter words so that the difference is more obvious, and vary the position of the odd one out.

Changing roles

A good way of helping children to learn is to ask them to be the one who sets the task or asks the questions – let them take over the adult role. From this position the child gets a better understanding of what's involved. Try changing roles in the activities that follow, after you've played them a few times.

years

Tapping and Clapping

Either tapping (with a wooden spoon on a cake tin) or clapping, you tap out a number of beats and then ask the child to repeat the rhythm. Start with just two or three beats and concentrate on getting the number right first. Then do gentle ones, then LOUD ones. Go on to see if they can copy a rhythm (LOUD – quiet – LOUD, or QUICK – QUICK – SLOW).

Vary the length and pattern. Most children won't be able to manage more than five beats but there are plenty of variations possible within this. When they've got the idea, ask them to tap or clap patterns for *you* to copy.

Clapping Syllables

Work from a picture book – for example, a book of zoo animal pictures which will give a good mix of syllables with words children are likely to know and find interesting.

Go through the book with the child, asking them to name the animals. Show them how to clap the syllables: CHIM-PAN-ZEE, etc. and then say: 'Let's do it together.'

SYLLABLES

Later on at school, when children are mastering phonics in reading and spelling, they will be taught that long words can be broken up into smaller units called syllables. If you can read or spell the syllables, you can often read or spell the whole word. Syllables have a rhythm (which is why they're basic to rhymes and songs) and children can be helped to become aware of this preschool; a valuable preparation for more formal work when they're at school.

Making Pastry Letters

You can do this with Play-Doh®, but somehow the whole business of mixing the pastry, rolling out the shapes and baking them in the oven gives it an extra dimension.

A good first stage is to make and bake the first letters of everyone's name (which they will then have to eat with pleasure, real or simulated).

Again it is the *activity* where they have to make up the letter that directs the child's attention to the details of the letter shapes.

SEEING THE DIFFERENCE

Letters

Letters are like very small diagrams with tiny differences between them. In learning to read we become able to notice these tiny differences in thousandths of a second. It takes time to get to that point, though!

Letters differ from each other in one or more detail; each detail is called a *distinctive feature*. The more distinctive features, the easier it is to tell letters apart. For example, *o* and *c* have only one difference (the gap); *o* and *e* have two differences (the gap and the loop back).

Words

Children learn to tell the difference between words first by noticing that some are longer than others or have a different shape, and only gradually by noticing the differences between the letters that make up the words. Encouraging a child to look at the letters is a way of getting them to look more closely at the words.

Matching Shapes

The progression is: picture shapes to geometric shapes to letter shapes. Picture shapes are easiest, but at this stage the child is also learning the matching game.

You make up a card with six different outline drawings of common objects/animals and six separate cards with the same drawings on them (a photocopier helps). The child has to match the drawings on the big card. Most children find this quite easy. If so, move on more quickly to geometric shapes, e.g.

Tell the child the correct *names* for the shapes. This makes it easier for them because they will usually want to talk themselves through the matching ('The triangle goes on the triangle', and so on).

When this becomes easy, move on to the basic letter shapes (*b, p, o, v, s, m, t, g*), telling the child the *sounds* for each letter. Start with just three letters.

Matching Letters to the Child's Name

This is a good activity to do with magnetic letters on the fridge door (they stay in place well and you can leave the result on display).

Write the child's name on a big piece of card and fix it in place. You put the initial capital letter under their name and then help them to find the other letters one by one. Letter cards with Blu-Tack on the back are an alternative to magnetic letters.

Alphabet Scrapbook

top ten

Like so many things that are successful with young children, this is very simple.

You will need: a *large* scrapbook, each page labelled with the capital and small version of each letter of the alphabet.

Then, with the child, you browse through magazines, comics and catalogues looking for suitable pictures to cut out – *just one or two initial-letter sounds at a time.*

You will almost certainly have to do the cutting out, but let the child do the sticking in, using a small glue stick.

Some children will want to do drawings as well.

Plastic letters and their uses

A set of plastic letters with small magnets in the back are one of the most useful things you can buy. A tub of 100 *lower-case* letters is not expensive. A brightly coloured tinned steel tray makes a good background (and keeps them together). The magnets mean that the letters are not easily dislodged.

Plastic letters have an enormous number of uses and, because they are *cut out* and fun to handle, children learn a lot about letter shapes from them.

Sounds and Letters

Matching Words by Their First Letter

Matching a word by its first letter draws the child's attention to that very important cue.

Using letters that look very different, lay out four or five plastic letters in a row.

Then give the child five *word* cards (one to match each initial letter) and show them how to line them up. Position the word card so that the initial letter of the word card is *exactly* under the corresponding plastic letter. Then muddle the word cards up and ask the child to match them.

When the child finds this easy, give them five new word cards (*different* word cards, *same* initial letters).

Later, move on to different groups of letters.

Peepholes

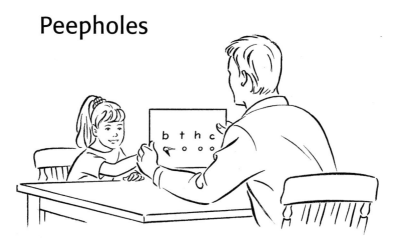

Children find this activity very enjoyable, which justifies the effort required to make the materials. Make up a card with pictures of four objects having different initial sounds. Under each picture cut a small hole (the peephole) big enough for the tip of a pencil to go through: a hole-punch is best for this. On the other side of the card, over each hole, write the initial-letter sound corresponding to each picture.

Hold the card up, picture side towards the child, and say: 'Which one begins with ____?' The child puts the tip of their pencil through the hole and you can check without seeing the picture.

Letter names and sounds

Each letter has a name and a sound. Teachers prefer children to learn sounds rather than names to begin with. Notice two things: that sometimes the 'name' is also another sound, and that saying a letter sound in isolation distorts it a bit.

Letter	Name	Sound	As in . . .
a	ay	ah	apple
b	bee	buh	butter
c	see	cuh	cake
d	dee	duh	duck
e	ee	eh	egg
f	eff	fuh	fish
g	gee	guh	gorilla
h	aych	huh	hair
i	eye	ih	insect
j	jay	juh	juice
k	kay	kuh	kick
l	ell	luh	love
m	em	muh	monkey
n	en	nuh	nut
o	oh	o	orange
p	pea	puh	pudding
q	kew	kw	queen
r	are	ruh	run
s	ess	suh	soap
t	tee	tuh	toffee
u	you	uh	umbrella
v	vee	vuh	van
w	double you	wuh	window
x	ecs	cs	xylophone
y	why	yuh	yo yo
z	zed	zuh	zoo

This Word Begins with . . .

Ask, for example, 'What does *baby* begin with?' If your child doesn't get it right away, say: 'It begins with *buh*. What does *boat* begin with?'

It's most likely to work first time if you start with words from the child's Word Book (p. 50).

As they get more confident, follow up by asking: 'Tell me another word that begins with _____.'

I Spy

This is the traditional game: 'I spy with my little eye, something beginning with . . .' Start with just three or four simple pictures or toys. Gradually expand the number of pictures or toys, so that the child has to do more searching. Don't forget to give *them* a chance to say 'I Spy . . .'

The next stage involves more searching. You need the kind of picture (perhaps in a book) where there are a large number of easily identifiable objects/animals/people. When you say 'I Spy', the child has not only to look carefully but to check off initial sounds in their head.

Finally you move on to the game we all know . . . It can be played in any room in the house, or in the garden. It helps if you set things out a bit, perhaps by making them a little more obvious. Otherwise it may prove too difficult and frustrating for the child. Later on, you can try it on a train or car journey, where they have to be quicker off the mark.

Matching Letters to Picture Words

For this you will need pictures with single words underneath; start with the child's Word Book (see p. 50). You then need separate plastic letters – or letters on separate pieces of card. Show the child how you make up the word from left to right, checking one letter at a time. This is simpler if the letters in the word are the same size as the separate letters – in which case, it is easier for the child to line them up.

LETTERS AND SOUNDS COMING TOGETHER

To begin with children learn about letters, and the sounds in words, separately. Letters are like small shapes or diagrams: children have to learn to see the difference before they can learn which sounds they stand for. And they can make a lot of progress in listening to the *sounds* that make up words before they learn to match sounds to letters – which is known as *phonics*.

PHONICS

Phonics involves teaching the sounds for each letter, or combination of letters, so that children can break down unknown words, sound them out and blend the sounds together. It all sounds very simple, and it would be if all letters had just one sound and all sounds had just one letter.

The phonic analysis of words is an important stage in teaching children to read, but one that should certainly be left until a child has started school and has made progress in independent reading. It is not something to be tackled at the preschool stage.

However, by teaching *initial*-letter sounds you are preparing your child for phonics, and in a particularly useful way: when a child is starting to read they can often guess what a word is in a sentence by recognizing what sound it begins with.

Copying Over Letters

For a young child, copying over individual letters is an easier 'complete' task than copying over whole words, which can seem a bit of a marathon.

But the activity needs to be *meaningful*, perhaps as part of making the Alphabet Scrapbook (see p. 97), or an alphabet frieze – very satisfying because it can 'grow' round the walls of the child's bedroom.

Use a highlighter pen and show the child where to start (with a starting dot) and which direction to go in (see p. 53).

For young children, this is a task that requires a great deal of attention, which is exactly why it has an important place in any programme of learning to read. To do a good job the child has to look at the letter shape very carefully indeed, and then follow it with their fingers – it is not done by eyes alone.

Using a Word Processor

Young children have always been fascinated by typewriters – even if they did get the keys tangled up! But typewriters are now virtually a thing of the past. In any case, at the level of putting up words and letters a word processor is much easier to use – and the results are shown up on what looks like a small television screen.

Partly it's the mechanics and technology of the thing, and partly it's the vivid, immediate and 'high-quality' result.

The focus is on letters building up words. You will need to supervise and correct mistakes – but children will happily copy words, and even sentences, letter by letter. They do this with great concentration, and this is where the learning comes in.

If you have a printer you can print out the child's products – either to make up a home-produced storybook, or to label a drawing, or simply as a record of achievement pinned up in the kitchen.

Matching Pictures by Initial Sound

You need:

- a card with six small pictures on it (similar to the one on p. 104), and

- six small separate pictures – different from those on the card, but matching the letter sounds.

Go over the pictures on the card with the child, asking: 'What's that? What sound does it start with?' Prompt them if necessary.

Then say: 'I've got some other pictures here and we're going to put them on the pictures that start with the same sound. Look, I'll show you.'

Get them to name the picture and give you its initial sound. Then say: 'Which picture on the card starts with a _____? [Pause] Right, so we put this little picture on top of it.'

Work through all six cards in this fashion, then gather them up and say: 'Now you do it on your own.' Come to the rescue if you need to.

Confusing letters

If you make letter cards you may find that your child has difficulty getting some of them in the right position or *orientation*. This can be a problem with plastic letter sets as well.

The 'problem' letters are these:

u n p q d b m w

because if they are turned round or upside down they look like a different letter.

b and *d* confusion is the biggest problem (see p. 111) and you have to work at that. But, in the meanwhile, you can make life a bit simpler for the child: on cards you can simply put a pencil line at the bottom (telling the child what this means); on plastic letters you can put a dot of white correction fluid at the bottom.

Of course, not all children find this a difficulty.

years

Matching Words by Their First Letter

Focusing children's attention on the initial letters of the word is something you can usefully do even if they don't know the sounds. It makes them *look*.

1   Pick words with simple first–letter sounds like *cat, purse, sock*, rather than words like *chin, sleep, photo*.

2   Choose three initial letters that look and sound very different to begin with: *s, t* and *m*, for example.

3   Make up four or five word cards for each letter, including words of very different length.

4   Set out three of the different word cards in a row.

5   Say to the child: 'I want you to put all the cards under this one that begins with *s* [say the *sound*], all the ones under this one that begin with *t*, and all the ones that begin with *m* under the last one. Look, I'll do the first one for you. Now you try.'

6   If they make a mistake, show them how you hold the card against each one in turn, saying: 'Is that the same letter?', etc.

Later on you can make the game more difficult by including letters that are more easily confused (like *m, n* and *u*).

Matching Letters to Pictures

This is quite a difficult task for young children, but one that they find very enjoyable, as it gives them a real sense of achievement. The child who can do this is well on the way to reading.

Make up a big card with six pictures (no words) from the now very familiar Word Book and six corresponding plastic letters. The child has to put the matching initial letter on the correct picture. To do this, they have to:

- name the picture

- think of the initial sound

- pick out the letter for that sound.

When the child can do this confidently, keep the number of pictures the same but give them more letters to choose from.

Matching Sets of Pictures by Their Initial-Letter Sounds

This activity is a bit more complicated.

1   Get together sets of pictures (mount each one on card of the same size) for these letters: *b, d, f, g, h, l, m, n, p, s, t* – all consonants, and not too difficult to find pictures for (an old mail-order catalogue is a good source, as well as magazines). You need a set of pictures (four or five) for each initial sound.

2   Work on three initial-letter sounds at a time, picking ones that are very different – like *b, s* and *t*.

3   Set out three pictures in a row and say: 'You see these pictures? What's this one . . . and this . . . and this? [Pause] Good. Now *baby* begins with *b*, and *soap* begins with *s*, and *train* begins with *t*.'

4   Say: 'Now look at these other pictures. [Spread them out.] Can you see another one that begins with *b*? . . . Good. We'll put that one under *baby* because it starts with the same sound', and so on.

5   Talk them through the first three and then say: 'Now you do it with these other pictures.' Emphasize that they check off just one picture at a time.

Finger-Writing

This is a good activity for getting letter shapes linked to sounds firmly in a child's mind.

Our knowledge of a letter shape is as much a matter of *feel* as sight. People who have *become* blind as adults can still write, although they sometimes overrun a bit (but even this improves with practice).

Getting children to write with their fingertip seems to fix the letter shape more firmly in their mind. Dyslexic children are often helped by this method – especially 'visual dyslexics' (see p. 65).

What you do is simple:

1   Show the child how you can 'write' a letter on a tabletop with your finger.

2   Get them to do it with you at the same time, talking it through ('Down and round', etc.).

3   Then ask them to do it on their own.

If children need to 'see' the result at first, you can put some sand or flour on a small tray – but move on from that. The next stage is when you ask the child to close their eyes and do it. Last of all, get the child to write the letters in the air. When they can do that, they've really got it.

Start with letter sounds they're sure about, then move on to the more problematic ones.

Letters Across the Room

This is a very acceptable activity for young children, or those who have had enough of working at the table – a good reserve activity or one for finishing off a session.

1   Make up big letter cards (A4 size) and prop up half a dozen round the room.

2   Hold the child next to you and say: 'I'm going to say the sound of a letter and I want you to run and touch it. Ready?'

IS PHONICS NECESSARY?

The short answer is: NO. Children can learn to read without being taught any phonics at all – although naturally good readers seem to work it out for themselves.

Nor does phonics teaching guarantee that children will read; there are plenty of non-readers who can sound out words perfectly well. More worrying is that you can find children who are almost disabled by phonics teaching – they get themselves into a most incredible muddle when they try to sound out and blend words.

And, to top it all, the most famous reading programme of recent times – Marie Clay's Reading Recovery programme – doesn't use systematic phonics, and deliberately has a reading-for-meaning emphasis.

But the fact remains that children generally do better if they have *some* phonics teaching. The emphasis in this book is on helping children to get the *beginning*-letter sounds as an aid to recognition, and breaking words up into syllables.

Because English is an 'alphabetic' written language, where letters correspond more or less to sounds, it's easy to assume that that has to be. But some languages are not alphabetic. In Chinese, for example, written words bear no 'sound' relationship to their spoken equivalent. Mandarin and Cantonese (the two main Chinese languages) use the same written words, but a Mandarin speaker can't understand a Cantonese speaker and vice versa. However, they can write to each other . . .

First-Letter Sounds

Collect a set of pictures from magazines of words that begin with simple letter sounds – not those that begin with two-letter sounds (like *th* and *ch*) or subtle blends (like *st* and *cl*), but words like *toe*, *window, fork, moon, jug.*

1   Spread out half a dozen pictures at a time.

2   Point to each one in turn and ask the child: 'What sound does this start with?'

3   If they can't do it, say: 'It's a window, so it begins with . . . [pause to give them a chance to say it] *w*.'

4   Make a note of the sounds that cause them problems.

Simple Blending: Two-Letter Words

The easiest introduction to blending letters together is to start with *two-letter words* – those that start with the vowels *a*, *i*, *o* and *u*.

1   Make up letter cards for these four vowels and the consonants *f, m, n, p, s, t*. With these you can make:

at   an   as   am   it   in   if   is   of   on   up   us

2   Set out the initial vowel card first. Ask: 'What sound does that make?'

3   Then put the consonant card next to it and ask: 'And what sound does that make?'

4   Then ask: 'What word do they make when you sound them both together?' Show the child how to do it yourself first, and then say: 'Now you do it.'

5   Keep the vowel the same, but change the consonant card.

6   When they can say the two sounds separately and then blend them together, go through the words again and say: 'Now I want you to say the two sounds together right away.'

Sounds and Letters

At this point what children are learning is the important skill of treating the first two letters of a word as one sound. If they can get this fixed in their minds it will be a great help to them when they come to deal with longer words.

At almost seven, Rachel seems to have hit a ceiling in her reading progress. She feels stuck and is frustrated by it. Her teacher thinks that her lack of ability with phonics is holding her up. However, Rachel easily gets anxious and muddled when she tries to break up into sounds words she doesn't know.

Her mother concentrates on teaching her to sight-read very complicated words; to get the beginning sounds of words right; to break words up into syllables; to use context to predict what a word might be. This orderly routine seems to be paying off. A typical session for Rachel might include:

- *playing Finish the Gap, where there are words missing in a page from a book but the first two letters are given (p. 35)*

- *playing Words and Crosses (p. 111) for simple blending*

- *playing Syllable-Slicing (p. 82)*

- *doing Initial Blends and Digraphs (p. 114)*

- *using the Wordmaker (p. 112).*

Find the First Letter

This one is a bit more difficult because not only do they have to work out the initial sound of the word but they have to identify the corresponding letter as well.

- Use the same pictures as before (see p. 108) but provide plastic letters (although letter cards will do).

- Show the child how they have to say what the word begins with and then find the letter, putting the letter underneath the picture.

Catch the Letter

This is good for a quick end-of-session activity.

1 Tell the child you are going to call out ten words and they have to write down *the first letter*.

2 Give the child a sheet of paper and ask them to write the numbers 1 to 10 down the left-hand margin.

3 Choose ten words with *different* first letters that make simple sounds (*s*un not *sl*ip, for example).

4 The child writes down the first letter as you say the word. If they seem stuck, say the word again and ask: 'What does that begin with?'

Word Ladders

This is a game that makes children think hard about the letters that make up words.

You have one three-letter word at the top of the ladder and another one at the bottom.

Like this: **dog**   Which becomes: **dog**

          ____   **dot**

          ____   **cot**

          cat   **cat**

What the child has to do is change the top word into the bottom one by changing *only one letter at a time*, and each change must make a real word.

It's best to start with just one intermediate step:

pan   **hat**

____   **____**

cat   **jam**

You'll easily work out some others.

CONFUSING *b* AND *d*

Young children often confuse *b* and *d* when they're reading – and sometimes they even muddle them up with *p* and *q*. It doesn't mean there's something wrong with their perception of letters.

The actual *shape* of *b* and *d* and *p* and *q* is identical – if you turn them round. Otherwise, things in the world are the same whatever their position: a chair is a chair which ever way you turn it – including upside down.

It's worth *talking* about this to your child if it's a problem for them. A useful way of remembering the *b/d* difference is the word *bed*:

If you write the word, the child can draw a stick figure lying on it, with the two uprights as the bed ends.

Words and Crosses

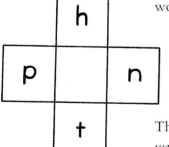

These are quick and easy to do, but give good practice in working out the sounds that make up three-letter words (and many long words are made up of these).

Make up an A4 sheet with about six cross shapes, as shown:

The child has to put in the vowel that will make a word *going both ways*. You'll easily be able to make up others. This is a good activity to finish a session with. It's also one where the child will need (or want!) very little help.

Sounds and Letters

years

The Wordmaker

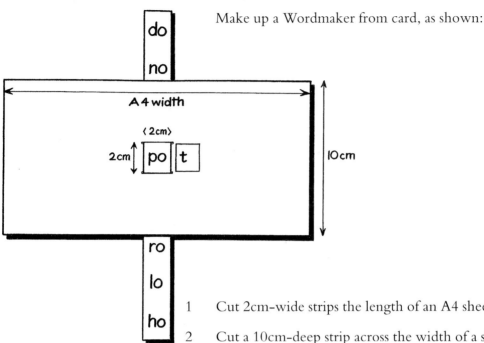

Make up a Wordmaker from card, as shown:

1   Cut 2cm-wide strips the length of an A4 sheet of card.

2   Cut a 10cm-deep strip across the width of a sheet of A4 card, i.e. one-third of a sheet.

3   Make two 2cm horizontal cuts, 2cm apart, just off centre. The long strips of card are going to run through this.

4   Make up a strip with the following consonant and vowel combinations:

no   co   po   do   ho   lo   fo   ro   go

They need to be big enough to fill the 2cm-high aperture.

5   Make up 2cm-square consonant cards as follows:

t   d   g   p

These you will mount next to the aperture with a piece of Blu-Tack. *But use only one of them in any one session.*

6   *Tell the child they have to say the first two letters together.* This stops any distortion from trying to sound the first two letters separately, then adding on the last letter (*po-t, co-t*, etc.).

top ten

7   Run the strip through, stopping only when the combination makes an actual word – although there is no harm in getting the child to say non-words like *fot*.

8   Do this a couple of times. Then ask the child to do it while *you* say the words; make a few errors so they have to correct you.

9   At the next session, change to a different final consonant and carry on as before.

When you've run through this series, focus on a different activity. Give the child all the necessary plastic letters and say: 'Now I'm going to say one of the words we've practised and I want you to make it up from these plastic letters.'

THEN GIVE THE CHILD A BREAK FROM THIS ACTIVITY. At weekly intervals you can repeat this sequence with the following combinations, making up the necessary strips:

- **su   tu pu nu bu**
  ru   cu gu hu
  with **n   m   t   p**

- **ha   ba ra sa ma**
  va   fa
  with **d   g   m   n   t**

- **pibi si di ri**
  wi   li
  with **n   t   g   d   b   p**

- **me   ge be de he**
  pe   se we
  with **t   n   d   m   g   b**

Each time, follow up with making words from that particular consonant/vowel combination using plastic letters.

All of this establishes a style and a framework for learning – into which you can then insert more difficult material: Initial Blends and Digraphs (see p. 114).

The Final 'E' Rule

Telling children to concentrate on the sounds made by the first two letters of a word works well in the main, but one big exception is when the word ends in *e*. This makes the vowel in the middle of the word (often the second letter) say its *name*.

It's probably worth concentrating to begin with on three-letter words + *e* so that it isn't too complicated. The following list provides enough material.

bit	cap	cod	dam	fad	fin
hat	hid	hop	kit	mad	man
mat	mop	not	pan	pin	pip
rat	rid	rip	rob	rod	tap
tub	win				

Put the three-letter words on cards – half a dozen at any one time – and ask the child to read them. Then present the same words again, but adding an *e* at the end, reminding them of the rule.

Initial Blends and Digraphs

Blends and digraphs are two letters that, said together, make a rather different sound from the two letters said separately. If the sound is *entirely* different, they're called digraphs (see p. 115).

Teach these by making up sets of cards of initial blends and digraphs and two- or three-letter endings – see page 119. Keeping the blend or digraph the same, change the endings and ask the child to read the words. When this is fluent, ask them to make up words you say from the cards.

Start with blends, which are easier than digraphs, taking three or four initial blends, and four or five endings. For example:

Blends	cr	fl	pr	sh
Endings	am	ed	ip	op	int

The fact that some combinations don't make real words doesn't matter. You can ask: 'Is that a word?'

Initial blends and digraphs and endings

These are the most important initial consonant blends and digraphs. The two- and three- letter endings will make up words (and non-words!) that the child will not find too difficult to read.

Digraphs

ch	ph	sh	th	wh

Blends

bl	br	cl	cr	dr
fl	fr	gl	gr	pl
pr	sc	sl	sm	sn
sp	st	sw	tr	

Endings

ab	ack	ad	ag	am
amp	an	and	ank	ass
at	ed	en	end	ent
ep	ick	ill	im	in
ing	ink	int	ip	irt
it	ock	og	one	op
ot	oto	ow	um	ump

WHY THE FIRST TWO LETTERS IN A WORD ARE SO IMPORTANT

There are two reasons:

■ If you get the first two letters right you can usually guess the rest from context.

■ Quite often the first two letters together make a sound quite different from the two letters sounded separately.

These are the most important two-letter sounds:

ch ph sh   wh th

(there are two ways of saying this last one)

They are known as *digraphs*. There are also a larger number of consonant blends where the two letters are still recognizable but merge into each other (like *cr*, *fl*, *sc*, *gl*, and so on; see p. 115). The rule is to tell the child always to pronounce the first two consonants of a word together, and also consonant/vowel beginnings when there's only one vowel (as in *window*); this also works when the order is vowel/consonant (as in *artist*). The rule doesn't work when you get two vowels together after the initial consonant (as in *wood* or *sound*).

Silent Highlights

This is a useful activity for the odd five minutes.

From the list in the 'Silent letters' box (see p. 117), write a dozen or so words containing silent letters on an A4 sheet, then mix them up. Write the words quite big. Give the child a highlighter pen and ask them to mark the silent letters in each word.

Silent letters

Silent letters – letters in a word you don't pronounce – are a problem for children who are using simple phonics. They need to be able to recognize them when they see them. Here are the most common ones:

Silent *b*

debt, lamb, climb, comb, bomb, crumb, plumber

(Note that they usually come after an *m* and at the *end* of words.)

Silent *k*

knee, know, knock, knob, knit, knife, knot, knight.

(The rule is simple: *kn* sounds as *n*.)

Silent *w*

wring, wreck, wrestle, wrist, wriggle, wrap, write, wrong, wrinkle (simple: *wr* sounds as *r*). But *wh* usually sounds the *w* (*what, where, when, which, whale, wheat, wheel, while, whine, white, why*), except when it's followed by *o*, when you sound the *h* (*whose, who, whole*).

Silent *gh*

night, caught, bright, light, sight, fight, tight, weight, eight, straight, except for *ghost* and when it forms part of *ough*, when it makes five sounds (*bough, cough, through, enough, thought* – see p. 122).

Silent *t*

listen, whistle, thistle, castle

Beginnings, ends and middles: vowel pairs

Vowel pairs (like *oo* and *oa*) mostly come in the middle of words. They are not difficult to deal with, but children can easily get confused. The rules are quite simple:

oo ⎫	can both be said two ways – as in *cook* and *boot*
ea ⎭	as in *bean* and *dead*
ay ⎫	
ai	
ee ⎬	easy – you just say the name of the first letter
oa ⎭	
oi	you say *oy*
ie	says the name of the first vowel (as in *lie*) or the second vowel (as in *chief*)
ou	says *ow* except when it comes before *gh* or *ld*
ow	says *ow* except when it says *oh*

Pick the Digraph

Make up an A4 sheet with these digraphs in boxes at the top:

ch   ph   sh   th   wh

On the rest of the page write ten to twenty words that take these beginnings but with a gap for the first two letters like this:

__ank   __oto   __ampoo

The child has to write in the digraph that makes a word. (See the list of digraph words opposite.) There are alternatives for some words but usually there's an obvious best fit.

Digraph words

You can use a dictionary, of course, but the following list contains the most common consonant digraphs at the beginning of words:

th (hard)

than, that, then, their, them, there, these, this

th (soft)

thank, thaw, thick, thief, thigh, thimble, thin, thing, think, third, thirst, thirty, thorn, thousand, thread, three, thrill, throat, throw, thumb, thunder

sh

shake, shall, shampoo, shape, shark, sharp, shave, shed, sheep, sheet, shelf, shine, ship, shirt, shock, shoe, shop, shoot, short, shot, show, shut

wh

whale, what, when, wheat, wheel, where, which, while, whip, whisper, white

ph

not many *common* words begin with this but it often occurs *in* words: pheasant, phone, photo, physics

ch

chain, chair, chalk, challenge, champion, change, channel, chapter, charity, chase, cheap, cheat, check, cheer, cheese, cherry, chess, chest, chestnut, chew, chicken, chief, child, chill, chimney, chin, china, chip, chocolate, chop, choose, church (but note that quite often the *h* is silent: chemist, Christmas)

The Long and Short Game

Both *oo* and *ea* have a long and a short sound.

1   Make up an A4 sheet with these words in boxes at the top:

moon	pool	bead	head
look	soot	mean	tread
foot	shoot	heap	dream
cool	hood	bread	threat

2   Add these columns at the bottom:

cook	boot	bean	dead
____	____	____	____
____	____	____	____
____	____	____	____

3   Read the words at the top of the columns, emphasizing the long or short sound.

4   Ask the child to write the words underneath that sound the same.

Highlighting Vowel Pairs

This is a very good activity for encouraging children to search *inside* words.

1   Photocopy a couple of pages from a book suitable to your child's level.

2   Write these vowel pairs at the top: *ay, ai, ee, oa, oi.*

3   Ask the child to highlight them whenever they occur.

Picture Pairs

This is not as easy a task as it looks: children really have to think about how words are made up. It works well because they enjoy it and don't realize how hard they're having to think.

1   Cut out pictures for words that contain these vowel pairs (arrow the important part of the picture if necessary):

> *oi*   point coin oil
>
> *ay*   tray spray hay
>
> *ai*   paint rain sail chain
>
> *ee*   feet sheep heel
>
> *oa*   coat toast

2   Mount the pictures in random order on an A3 sheet (or two A4 sheets taped together).

3   Write the vowel pairs in a line at the top.

4   Ask the child to write down the correct vowel pair under each picture.

I or *E*?

Children need to be clear that when you say the *ie* combination you either say the name of the *i* or the name of the *e*. Once they've grasped that, they'll usually get it right.

1   Make up an A4 sheet with ten or more words from these two lists:

> *silent* e   lie cried pie fried tied tried
>
> *silent* i   chief thief belief piece grief
>   believe relief field shield

2   Ask them to highlight the silent letter in each case.

Sounds and Letters

7 ▶
years

How Now Brown Cow?
or Sow, Grow and Mow

A simple activity fixes the two ways of saying *ow* in a child's mind.

1   Put these words in a box at the top of an A4 sheet:

sow	**clown**	**tow**	**how**	**brown**
grow	**flown**	**mow**	**now**	**frown**

2   Add these columns
     at the bottom.

cow	**low**
——	——
——	——
——	——
——	——
——	——

3   Read the words at the top of
     the columns, emphasizing the
     sound. Then say to the child:
     'Now you write these words
     in the box under the words
     that sound the same.'

8 ▶
years

Rough Enough

Ough is the most troublesome group of letters in the English language. Children have to learn to *look out* for it.
There are five ways of saying *ough*:

bough says bow   **enough says enuff**
cough says coff   **thought says thawt**
though says thoh

Write these words, well spaced out on a large sheet of paper and, with the child, think together of other *ough* words that are sounded in these different ways.
You'll both have to work at it — and the child will benefit!

Sounds and Letters

Last words

Where do you go from here?

SO YOUR CHILD CAN READ. But that's only a beginning.

We have two problems with literacy:

- children (and adults) who can't read anywhere near adequately (and the number runs into millions), and

- children (adults ditto) who can read but don't.

Once you can read you don't lose it. But to become a really skilled reader, to become really literate, you need practice. Lots and lots of practice. This is true of any skill: tennis, drawing, playing the piano . . . People who are really good at these things have worked at it over and over for months and years.

Good readers are always reading: for them, books are almost a drug. They get faster and it becomes effortless. One of the reasons literacy standards are falling is that children spend *less time* reading.

Being able to *write* follows on slowly from this practice, but it is also a separate skill. One doesn't guarantee the other. To learn how to write you have to practise writing. Not many people do that; not many people are professional writers.

You can't make children read, but if you study their tastes and interests you can buy or borrow books that might suit them. And if they show a liking for a particular author then you can get more of them. Second-hand books, particularly those in charity shops, are amazingly cheap. There's no reason why they shouldn't be part of your routine shopping round.

Helping your child doesn't stop when they've achieved a basic literacy competence. You may feel that you need further help or want to find out more. The following addresses are for organizations that can provide a range of further information and support – for example, details of children's book clubs and specialized assessment and teaching services.

Useful addresses

In the USA and Australia, individual states have considerable autonomy so that school systems and education services, including help for children with reading difficulties, vary from one to another. This applies to the *voluntary* sector as well: information has to be obtained locally. The addresses of national-level voluntary organizations are given below.

United Kingdom

Book Trust
Book House
45 East Hill
Wandsworth
London SW18 2QZ
Tel: (0181) 870 9055
Fax: (0181) 874 4790
This is the main charity for books and reading in the UK. Children's books receive special attention via The Story Book Trust.
It has an excellent information service and is well worth a visit if you live in London (and even if you don't). It also has a wide range of special publications – including *YBT News*.

Book Trust Scotland
Scottish Book Centre
137 Dundee Street
Edinburgh EH11 1BG
Tel: (0131) 229 3663
Fax: (0131) 228 4293
BT Scotland has a particular emphasis on children's books and has a comprehensive display of those recently published – bookshops only have a very restricted range.

Federation of Children's Book Groups
Secretary: Alison Dick
6 Bryce Place
Currie
Edinburgh EH14 5LR
Tel: (0131) 449 2713
A voluntary organization for all those interested in children's books. Many local groups are affiliated. It also publishes an annual list of best children's books chosen for the Children's Book Award.

The National Literacy Trust
Swire House
59 Buckingham Gate
London SW1E 6AJ
Tel: (0171) 828 2435
Fax: (0171) 931 9986
Works with a wide range of agencies to enhance reading standards in the UK as well as encouraging reading for pleasure. It publishes a journal, *Literacy Today*, which carries a wide range of news and information.

United States

The Children's Literacy Initiative (CLI)
c/o Linda Katz
320 Walnut Street
Philadelphia
PA 19106
Tel: (215) 574 2920
Fax: (215) 574 1404
This organization was founded in 1988, and provides a range of services targeted mainly on young children in low-income families. It provides training for parents and professionals, organizes summer reading programmes, produces radio programmes and publishes practitioner manuals.

The Barbara Bush Foundation for Family Literacy (BBFFL)
Executive Director:
Bentia Somerfield
1002 Wisconsin Avenue NW
Washington
DC 20007
Tel: (202) 338 2006
Fax: (202) 337 6754
BBFFL was founded in 1989 with the aim of establishing literacy as a family value and breaking the inter-generational cycle of illiteracy in American families. It supports a wide range of initiatives and produces a number of publications.

Australia

The International Board of Books for Young People
North Terrace
Adelaide
South Australia
SA 5000
Tel: (8) 8207 7259
Fax: (8) 8207 7351

How to get help for your child

All education systems have a psychology service, although they work in different ways. Your local education office will be able to give you the address and telephone number if you want to contact it direct. National and local government services are normally free. However, if you feel that your child's difficulties are not being acknowledged you could get in touch with the local or national Dyslexia Association.

United Kingdom

British Dyslexia Association
98 London Road
Reading RG1 5AU
Tel: (0118) 966 8271

Scottish Dyslexia Association
Unit 3
Stirling Business Centre
Wellgrain
Stirling FK8 2DZ
Tel: (01786) 446650
These charities coordinate a large number of local associations all over the country. They can put you in touch with your nearest one. Do bear in mind that this is not normally a free service.

United States

The Orton Dyslexia Society
Chester Building
Suite 382
8600 La Salle Road
Baltimore
MD 21286 2044

Tel: (410) 296 0232
Fax: (410) 321 5069

Learning Disabilities Association (LDA)
4156 Library Road
Pittsburgh
PA 15234
Tel: (412) 341 1515
Each state in the USA has its own policy on dyslexia and this is further complicated by individual state laws. It follows that there are different standards for who does and does not get services. In the USA, the term 'learning disability' is used differently from its UK meaning. Many American parents do not consider dyslexia to be a learning disability in the UK sense.

Australia

SPELD NSW Inc
129 Greenwich Road
Greenwich
NSW 2065
Tel: (2) 9906 2977
Fax: (2) 9906 5657

SPELD QLD Inc
72 Cornwall Street
Annerley
QLD 4103
Tel: (7) 3217 4455
Fax: (7) 3217 4456

SPELD Victoria Inc
494 Brunswick Street
Fitzroy
VIC 3068
Tel: (3) 9489 4344
Fax: (3) 9486 2437

SPELD SA Inc
298 Portrush Road
Kensington
SA 5068
Tel: (8) 8431 1655
Fax: (3) 9486 5751

Dyslexia – SPELD
PO Box 409
South Perth
SA 6851
Tel: (9) 474 3494
Fax: (9) 367 1145

SPELD ACT Inc
c/o Shout Office
PO Box 717
Mawson
ACT 2607
Tel: (6) 290 1984
Fax: (6) 286 4475

SPELD Tasmania
PO Box 154
North Hobart
TAS 7002
Tel: (02) 6234 8489
The term 'specific learning difficulty' is generally preferred to the term 'dyslexia' in educational circles in Australia.

New Zealand

SPELD New Zealand Inc
PO Box 27
122 Wellington
New Zealand
There are thirty-five SPELD branches in New Zealand, each with a branch president and local committee. As in Australia, 'dyslexia' is not the generally accepted term.

Book clubs

These are book clubs for children in the UK. Library services in the USA, Australia and New Zealand can provide information about national book clubs.

Discovery: The Book Club for Children
Book Club Associates
87 Newman Street
London W1P 7EN
Tel: (0171) 637 0341
Fax: (0171) 291 3525
BCA is the largest book club organization in the UK and most of the clubs you've ever heard of are part of it.

Books for Children
Time-Life Entertainment
Group Ltd
4 Furseground Way
Stockley Park
Uxbridge
Middlesex UB11 1DP
Tel: (0181) 606 3061
Fax: (0181) 606 3099
Part of a 'family book' service.

Letterbox Library
Children's Book
Co-operative
Unit 20/2nd Floor
Leroy House
436 Essex Road
London N1 3QP

Concentrates on promoting non-sexist, multicultural books for children of all ages.

Red House Book Clubs
Cotswold Business Park
Witney
Oxford OX5 8YT
Tel: (01993) 774171/771144
Fax: (01993) 776 813
Four different clubs selling directly to parents, and through Book Parties as well as Scholastic and Red House School Book Clubs.

So you want to know more about children's literacy?

Many parents who have helped their own child find that they want to know about how children learn to read, how they can be taught (many different opinions!) and about children's books in general.

Here are a few key books, which you can usually get from your local library on interlibrary loan:

Adams, Marilyn (1991) *Learning to Read*, Boston, MA: MIT Press.
The best survey of reading research ever published. Detailed, intelligent and remarkably easy to read.

Butler, Dorothy (1987) *Cushla and Her Books*, Harmondsworth: Penguin (previously published by The Bodley Head, 1979).
A sensitive and thought-provoking account of how a child with language and learning difficulties developed in response to favourite picture storybooks.

Clarke, Margaret (1976) *Young Fluent Readers*, London: Heinemann.
A fascinating account of children who learned to read before starting school.

Hornsby, Beve and Shear, Frula (1993) *Alpha to Omega:*

The A–Z of Reading, Writing and Spelling, Oxford: Heinemann.
The completely opposite tack to Liz Waterland's book below. Part of a specialized programme, it is intended for use with the severely dyslexic. The most comprehensive phonics programme ever.

Waterland, Liz (1988) *Read with Me: An Apprenticeship Approach to Reading*, Stroud: The Thimble Press.
A remarkably sensible and sensitive account of an infant-school headteacher's approach to helping young children learn to read.

Index

Index